The Emmerdale Club

Celebrating 25 Years

by
Angie Stanger-Leathes

Published by Limelight Classic Productions Limited

First Published in Great Britain in 2016 by
Limelight Classic Productions Ltd, Fort House, Old Hartley, NE26 4RL

A catalogue record for this book is available from the British Library

ISBN – 978-0-9560392-7-9

Printed and bound in North Shields by yourPrintDepartment.co.uk

Limelight Classic Productions Ltd
Fort House
Old Hartley
NE26 4RL

www.limelightclassics.com

Introduction

The Emmerdale Story

'Emmerdale Farm' was first broadcast on 16th October 1972 and remains one of ITV's showpiece dramas. Produced by ITV Yorkshire and filmed in Leeds, the programme has been broadcast in every ITV region and was originally created by Kevin Laffan, who was asked to write episodes based on a farming family, using the background of the Yorkshire Dales as its magnificent setting. The village of Arncliffe was used as the original venue for the show and in 1975, the location was changed to Esholt in West Yorkshire. In 1978, having been initially broadcast in the afternoons, the show moved to early evening transmission and viewing figures really started to rise. The show's success meant that crowds flocked to the locations used for filming and it was decided the village needed to be a closed set. In 1998 on the Harewood Estate, just outside of Leeds, the village of Esholt was re-created and outside filming is done there to this day, with indoor scenes filmed at the ITV studios in Leeds.

The Sugden family and their farm were initially the main focus of the show and as more characters were introduced, it was decided to spread the focus more to village life. Amos Brearley was landlord of the village pub, 'The Woolpack', in those early years and other families, including the Glovers, joined the village setting. Many more characters were introduced over the years, and the show became a firm favourite across the ITV regions.

By the time the show celebrated its 21st anniversary in 1993, it had been transformed from a minor, daytime rural drama into a major UK 'soap'. In that year the show attracted its highest viewing audience (over 18 million) when tragedy struck the village in the form of a plane crash which killed 4 people. It was then that the villagers decided to change the name of their village from Beckindale to 'Emmerdale' to help them deal with the trauma. Throughout the 1990's, big character families were introduced including the Tates, the Dingles, the Reverend Ashley Thomas and his family, followed by the Kings in 2004, the Bartons and the Sharmas in 2009 and the White family in 2014.

In 2012 the show celebrated its 40th anniversary and in that year the first ever 'live' episode was broadcast featuring two marriages, a birth and an unexpected death. It was a defining moment for the show and one which proved how its popularity had endured over a considerable period of time.

Now in 2016, the show is aired five nights a week, attracting between 5 and 7 million viewers per episode with omnibus repeats on Saturdays and Sundays. The storylines are stronger than ever, tackling some hard hitting topics including dementia and child abuse. ITV are rightly proud of this wonderful show which covers so many different walks of life, and tribute must be paid here to the management, cast and crew who work tirelessly to keep the show consistently high in the TV ratings. As we go to print the show has just won 'Best Soap' in the 2016 TV Soap Awards. An honour totally deserved.

Matt Cleary is Head of Production and since joining Emmerdale in 2009, Matt has been a great supporter of Jenny and the fan club members, spending much time and effort making sure the club weekends are generously supported by the cast and crew. He told us: "The Emmerdale Club celebrated 25 years in 2015. We make the programme for people like you and we're boundlessly grateful to you for sticking with us, supporting what we do. Who knows what Emmerdale will be like in 25 years time? My gut feeling is that we will still be making it. There will still be Sugdens in it, but whether we'll be watching it on a television screen or some other technology remains to be seen. What I do know is that we'll still be producing the show for our fans, trying to entertain and surprise those who tune in. And hopefully the Emmerdale Club will be celebrating its 50th anniversary, and we will be raising a glass to all members past and present. But in the meantime … here's to the future …here's to Emmerdale … and here's to you all. Cheers!"

Matt Cleary, Head of Production at Emmerdale

Chapter 1

The Curtain Raiser

This opening chapter is written by the founder of the Emmerdale Fan Club, Jenny Godfrey. Jenny tells us in her own words how the dreams of a fan grew into a special club which is still thriving and has made dreams come true for hundreds of fans over the years.

"It has been and continues to be, a great pleasure running The Emmerdale Club, and it all started with a letter.

I have watched Emmerdale from the beginning and always loved it from that first episode. In the early 1980's, whilst visiting an aunt and uncle who had a farm near Harrogate, they told me the location of the village and farm used for filming. At that time, Yorkshire Television had an agreement with the residents not to disclose filming locations, but of course many viewers found them, including me.

I had the idea of a fan club but I was working full-time and not in a position to start one until the Summer of 1988. I was at home with two young children, when I wrote a letter to Producer Stuart Doughty. It took some convincing, but eventually I had a meeting in London with Stuart and Head of Publicity Sallie Ryle. They became receptive to the idea and there was a further meeting in Leeds with Stuart and Production Supervisor, Tim Fee.

In September 1989 Emmerdale had a press day to show the media around their new home, Sunny Bank Mills in Farsley. It was an old mill that had been converted to studios and it was full of atmosphere ... and a ghost. It was during this day it was announced that an Emmerdale fan club would be launched.

The club was launched at London Zoo in January 1990. Five of the cast, Stan Richards, Arthur Pentelow, Ronald Magill, Glenda McKay and Cy Chadwick came along with Tim, Stuart and Sallie. TV presenter James Whale and journalist Hilary Kingsley joined us as our first honorary members and the very first club members Pam and Derek Burleigh were among the invited guests and journalists. There was lunch and a press photo-call with an Asian elephant called Lyang-Lyang. It was the beginning of the only British 'soap' to have an official fan club.

Fan Club launch at London zoo: cast members L-R: Cy Chadwick, Ronald Magill, Arthur Pentelow, Stan Richards, Glenda McKay

From the very start I had a great ally in Tim Fee, who was very enthusiastic about a club. He was very supportive and was involved right up until he retired. He gave our members some fantastic, fun-filled Emmerdale experiences. He left a legacy to the club and its members, and we continue to benefit from his ideas and input to this day.

The first actor I met was Stan Richards who played Seth Armstrong. He was very kind to me and supportive of the club and he was also kind to my young boys, taking them into the Woolpack and sitting with them at the bar. Another cast member who was very nice to my boys was Richard Thorp who played Alan Turner. I remember one occasion when he sat them on his Harley Davidson motorbike and they were absolutely delighted. Richard loved bikes and often rode to work on his Harley.

When Matt Cleary, Head of Production, joined Emmerdale in 2009, he became my contact, along with Alli Piggott, Public Liaison Co-ordinator. They continue to open the Emmerdale doors to us for our exclusive, unique and fantastic fan club events. Along with cast and crew, they generously give up their time to give us a fun, interesting and informative weekend.

The club has brought me many unexpected pleasures. Shortly after our launch I was asked to do television and radio interviews. The first one was outside the original Emmerdale farmhouse and the second at the kitchen table with Sheila Mercier (Annie Sugden). Those first interviews were nerve wracking but exciting. I continued to do interviews and was then asked to be a TV critic on BBC 3 Counties radio which led to broadcasts on various BBC stations including Leeds and Belfast. One sticks out in my mind – a late night Radio Five Live programme and there was a live link to Alan Fletcher (Karl Kennedy in Neighbours). A couple of years later I was delighted to meet him when he was in the UK doing Pantomine and we still keep in touch.

I have been a big fan of Tony Hatch and the songs he co-wrote with Jackie Trent ever since I was a teenager and I bought all of Petula Clark's records.

Knowing he also wrote the show's theme tune, I contacted Tony and was delighted when he replied and wrote a piece for the club's newsletter. It continues to be a great pleasure to know Tony and when I unexpectedly saw Petula Clark in concert in Sydney (she was amazing), I immediately emailed Tony and told him how highly she spoke of him and his work.

When I went to Sydney I had the pleasure of meeting up with Emily Symons who played Louise Appleton in Emmerdale. She left the show to return to her native Australia and returned to 'Home and Away', reviving her character 'Marilyn'. I met her at the studios in her lunch break. She had agreed to be interviewed for the club newsletter and after coffee in the café, she said she was soon due back on set but would I like to look around the studios which was lovely and I got to meet Steve Peacock who played 'Brax'.

I also met Sir Peter Leitch from New Zealand who is an honorary member of our club and we chatted about Emmerdale over afternoon tea in London. A most interesting man who is a big fan of the show and visits the studios whenever he is in the UK.

When a club member told me he was going to Pinewood Studios for the unveiling of a blue plaque in honour of Sir John Mills, I told him I grew up two fields away from Sir John's home in Sussex, and have very fond memories of the family. He invited me to join his table and after the event I got to meet Hayley and Juliet Mills, who fondly remembered their time in Sussex. Juliet is married to Maxwell Caulfield, who played Mark Wylde in Emmerdale and it was good to see him again as he had recently left the show.

Kathleen Beedles who was Producer on Emmerdale from 2005 to 2008 was a great supporter of the club weekends. When she moved to BBC in 2011 to work on Eastenders, she very kindly invited me to lunch and a tour of Albert Square, and I felt really honoured that she did.

It has and continues to be a great pleasure seeing the children grow into adults and hearing about their life's journey. Judith and Neil Gregory were small children with their mum Jean and I've known Jack Burroughs since he was a little boy and now he has grown up, working in law and is also a writer. Margaret Morgan keeps me updated about her daughter Susan who is now a teacher and involved in amateur dramatics. Members have of course seen my sons Robert and Michael grow from small boys to men during the time I have been running the fan club.

When members tell me of the friends they have made through the club and refer to us as their 'Emmerdale family', it is so heartwarming and pleasing to know that such good friendships have been made between members.

From the onset, our Emmerdale weekends have been tremendously successful and over the years many of the crew have given up their weekends to be with us, showing us around and generously sharing with us their knowledge and giving us a good time. A special mention and thanks must be made here to Val Lawson, Prue Haynes and Roly Plant.

We also have social lunches, one in Leeds, one in London, and it is an opportunity for us all to meet up between club weekends. Members come from near and far, even some from overseas and some go to both. I am immensely proud of their loyalty and support.

Over the years we have recognized our milestone anniversaries by planting bushes and trees in the village. In 2015, I was very excited when Matt said he had arranged for a plaque to be placed on the Emmerdale Village Hall to acknowledge 25 years of the fan club. Furthermore there was an unveiling, followed by lunch. John Whiston, Managing Director of Continuing Drama, Gaynor Faye (Megan) and Chris Chittell (Eric) joined Matt, Alli, some crew and a few club members for a most memorable day. It means a great deal to me for Emmerdale to acknowledge the club in this special way. I was also presented with a framed keepsake which was most unexpected and an honour for me.

Emmerdale and television have changed so much over the years, but the club remains the same, a club for the fans and run by a fan. We are a community, regardless of age we all have something in common; our love of Emmerdale. There are members from the UK, Northern Ireland, Southern Ireland, Sweden, Finland, New Zealand, the USA and Canada. I feel privileged to be in contact with people from around the world and to spend time with some of them during our club events.

The success and longevity of the club is down to its members, without them there would be no club, and also to Matt, Alli, the cast and production team, past and present, I give a very big thank you. To Tim, Stuart and Sallie, who had faith in me and the idea of a club, a very special thank you to each and every one of you".

Chapter 2

The Early Days

The first members to join the club were Pam and Derek Burleigh. Pam was a great character and also a talented 'needlewoman'. She knitted and embroidered Emmerdale jumpers and cushions, and even made some kitchen curtains using Emmerdale tea towels! Pam and Derek attended many club weekends over the years and also cheered the team at cricket matches. In fact Pam had so much memorabilia, Derek had to build her a cabin in the garden to house it all.

The first members - Derek and Pam Burleigh

More members swiftly followed during that first year and 4 of them, June Brown Jenny Dutton, Susan Edwards and Margaret Morgan have fond memories they are happy to share:

June Brown: "That very first episode of Emmerdale Farm all those years ago certainly opened a number of different avenues in life for me. Country life was always of interest, so the show really was a different type of 'soap'. After a number of years watching every episode, I noticed in the press than an official fan club had been launched. I immediately put pen to paper and I joined. After a short while, I enrolled my cousin Bryan as a member too. Right from the very first newsletter we were hooked.

June Brown and Jenny Dutton with Emmerdale friends

At this point I would like to make it clear that had it not been for a very young mother, Jenny Godfrey, with two very young little boys, Robert and Michael, I would not be writing this. It was Jenny who sought permission to form a fan club and the now retired Tim Fee gave Jenny his full support, together with many other staff connected with the show, with a special mention to Alli Piggott, who has always been there for us. Club members range from babes in arms to much more senior ages – which I have been for a long time! The fans come from all walks of life and many true friendships have been made over the years. In the early days of the club, a day at Emmerdale was arranged for club members and some of us applied to attend. It was held at Farsley Studios near Leeds. We were taken on a tour and enjoyed a buffet lunch with cast members including Richard Thorp (Alan Turner), Clive Hornby (Jack Sugden) and Tony Pitts (Archie Brooks). It was a wonderful treat for us and was followed in time by more events and fan club weekends, the highlight always being the gala dinner when we get the chance to mix with the cast and crew who give up their social time to be with us all. I have made wonderful friends over the years and I am sure there are many members like me who want to say 'Thank you Emmerdale, thank you Jenny'. To celebrate 25 years of the fan club is marvellous".

Jenny Dutton: "I joined the fan club within the first few weeks of its launch and my first trip was to 'Sunny Bank Mills' after winning the newsletter competition for a day at Emmerdale. I remember standing at Annie's back door and the whole experience was a wonderful one.

When my husband Peter became a member we enjoyed many Sundays at the charity cricket matches and on occasions, stayed for the weekend. On one such weekend, June Brown, Norman and Irene Cooper, Peter and myself walked the footpath to the village – not very comfortable for Irene in her wheelchair. I took lots of photos and finished the film the next day only to find I had been snapping with an empty camera!

Peter and I took part in several 'shoots', one of which in December 1994 was Kim and Frank Tate's wedding at Ripon Cathedral. While filming took place, Peter and I were asked to walk along a nearby footpath and yes, there was a glimpse of us in that episode. The filming was followed by lunch in a marquee at the hotel before returning for more filming. The Cathedral was open to the public and there were many interested spectators as the filming of the ceremony took place in the choir stalls. I sat next to 'Betty'. The wedding reception was held at the hotel and we were given salad to eat on a stop-start basis so we always had something to eat as filming took place. We later waved the happy couple off on their honeymoon! There were approximately 10 club members there that day and we set off for home arriving around midnight, having had a long but very interesting day.

I met Sheila Mercier and Kevin Laffan at a special party weekend to celebrate 25 years of the show along with 3 other club members. It was a marvellous experience and I didn't go to bed until 5 a.m. after the party.

I have many happy memories and made many friends over the 25 years of the fan club and hope it will last for many more years".

Susan Edwards and her husband Robin were founder members during the first month of the club's launch. They have attended many club weekends and Susan has provided some lovely words dedicated to actors who have appeared in the show. "Over the years many well known actors have joined the cast. At the time of writing we still have Freddie Jones, a great actor who has appeared in many films, Patrick Mower who I first saw in the detective series 'Target' and Elizabeth Estensen of 'Liver Birds' fame. We must not forget either a young Chris Chittell in 'To Sir With Love'. I've also had the

pleasure to meet Richard Thorp, who I admired as a handsome young pilot in 'Dambusters'. Also as a young girl I watched 'The Silver Sword' on TV about a young boy during the war played by Frazer Hines. How pleased I was to meet him years later playing Joe Sugden, one of my favourite characters.

Susan Edwards with Bobby Knutt (Albert Dingle)

When actors leave Emmerdale they often work in theatre and sometimes appear at the Theatre Royal, Norwich. We've had Hayley Tammadon in panto as Cinderella, Lisa Riley and Deena Payne in 'Calendar Girls' and recently Ian Kelsey in 'Shawshank Redemption'. It's lovely to see how they progress, especially having met them when starting their careers on the set of Emmerdale".

Margaret Morgan: "We, as a family have been members of the club since

July 1990. My parents, Joan and Arthur Shaw, myself and my husband Steve and daughter Susan, went on our first visit to Esholt in the early 1990's and that visit also included watching the Emmerdale cricket team play against the local villagers. For several years we arranged our holidays in Yorkshire to co-incide with the cricket matches at Esholt. On one of these occasions, Jenny gave us an invitation to the Harewood Estate for the filming of a country fayre. We arrived early morning and to see everything that happens on a film shoot was an exciting and wonderful experience.

Our daughter Sue was delighted to be asked to walk a dog around a show-ring and appeared in the background in one of the scenes filmed that day. My husband Steve and my dad Arthur were chosen to walk out of the fayre behind the characters of Frank, Zoe and Kim (this was the scene which was shown just prior to Frank Tate having a heart attack). After it was shown on TV, my husband was shopping in a supermarket and a complete stranger came up and asked him if he had been on TV. Steve thought it was someone who knew we had been extras but it was quite genuine, the person really

Margaret Morgan and family

had recognised him from that episode. He must have a distinctive face! We laughed about that for quite a while. My parents have both passed away now but I know that our family have thoroughly enjoyed being club members and we would like to thank Jenny for all her help to make it possible – long may it continue".

Fan club membership rose swiftly in the next few years and by the show's 21st anniversary in 1993, the club was increasing in numbers on almost a weekly basis, echoing the increase in the show's popularity on screen. Great times were to follow for members during the next 20 plus years – and this book is dedicated to all of them.

Chapter 3

Precious Memories and Special Days

When Jean Gregory joined the club in 1992, it was to be the start of an annual journey to club weekends in Leeds for Jean and her young children. Judith and her brother Neil were the youngest members ever to be enrolled in the fan club, and also attend club weekends.

Judith (Jude) Gregory is happy to share her memories of special times with her mum at the weekends, spanning more than 20 years: "Emmerdale and the club weekends were a major part of my childhood. I have been attending them for more than 20 years, firstly when my mum Jean was still pregnant with me. Over the years my brother Neil and I always found something new to explore and every different weekend brought new experiences and new people to meet. Neil and myself have grown up with the Emmerdale cast and crew as well as members of the club. In more recent years Neil had not been able to attend the weekends but my mum and I still continued to enjoy them very much indeed.

Looking forward in anticipation of meeting new 'Emmerdale enthusiasts' each year and visiting the studios and the village, always brings excitement as there is always something new to find that we haven't seen before. Partying with the cast, crew and fellow members is always a highlight on the Saturday night after the gala dinner.

Jean (front) with Judith and Neil

Unfortunately my mum passed away in December 2014. It was a shock to everyone as it was so sudden. Mum was really looking forward to celebrating the fan club's 25th anniversary in 2015 and the Emmerdale weekends were always the highlight of the year for mum. Emmerdale was a huge part of her life – she watched the first ever episode and had never missed one since.

Judith and Neil with Mark Charnock

She used to visit Esholt with her mum and they would stand for hours watching the filming. When she first heard that a fan club had started she was thrilled and joined as soon as she could. I think I'm right in saying she was one of the longest standing members of the club".

Jude and her brother Neil attended the 25th club weekend celebrations and everyone in the club who ever met the family will know how much the club means to the Gregory family.

Jean with Tom Lister

Norman Cooper and his wife Irene were on holiday in West Yorkshire and saw a notice for a cricket match at Esholt between the Emmerdale 'All Stars' and the 'Bunbury XI'. When they arrived at the cricket ground they discovered that the game had been played a few weeks earlier but were given a souvenir programme with an advert inside for the fan club. Norman recalls: "We joined as soon as we could and our first club weekend was supposed to be in December 1995. Unfortunately Irene had a knee operation a month earlier, and her recovery did not go according to plan so we had to cancel. Sadly, Irene's health deteriorated and after that she needed to use a wheelchair.

Irene with Clive Hornby

Our first chance to savour the special atmosphere of a club weekend eventually came our way in January 1998 at the Weetwood Hotel in Leeds. I was delighted to meet my favourite cast member, Malandra Burrows (Kathy) on the Saturday evening and I had my photo taken with her. It was absolute heaven! On our table at the gala dinner we had Clive Hornby (Jack) and Richard Thorp (Alan), both sadly no longer with us. The next weekend we attended, our VIP guests at table were James Hooton (Sam) and Malandra Burrows (Kathy). I made sure I sat next to her and was starstruck all evening!

We have made some very dear friends over the years and they include June

Norman with Malandra Burrows

Brown, Bryan Dickson (sadly no longer with us), Geoff Dixon, Jenny Dutton, Susan Hartley and Steve Marshall, amongst others. In February 2008 Irene and I attended what was to be our last club weekend together. Irene was delighted to spend time chatting to Caroline Strong (Mel Doland) and have her photo taken too. Sadly Mel was the last cast member Irene met as she passed away 7 weeks later. My very last photo of Irene was taken outside the old Burley Road studios and it is one I will always treasure.

The following club weekend I knew would be very difficult but I was determined to attend and 3 club members rallied round and made sure I got through it. Thank you Jeanette Atherton, Margaret Cue and Elsie Stratford for your wonderful support. Charlotte Bellamy (Laurel) was also very kind to me that weekend. She had met Irene many times and was a wonderful comfort when she saw how emotional it was for me.

Irene outside ITV studios

I've now attended 18 weekends and the 25th anniversary celebrations were absolutely wonderful. Thanks to Jenny and the wonderful cast and crew for making the weekends so very special for the fans".

When Stan Richards passed away in 2005, the show lost one of its most colourful characters. Stan was a great supporter of fan club events and our founder Jenny recalls: "The first cast member I met was Stan Richards who played Seth Armstrong and he was very supportive of the club over the years. He attended his final club weekend in 2004 and although he was very ill, he was determined to be there and his daughter brought him to the hotel in a wheelchair. He said to me: 'Jenny, I am going to walk into

Stan Richards with Chris Pickering

dinner' - and he did. Stan donated a set of his precious pens to the auction as he wanted a fan to have them. In his memory we dedicated a wooden bench to Stan, which resides in the Emmerdale graveyard to this day".

Tim Fee also recalls a spooky incident as the fans gathered around the bench for a dedication to Stan: "Just as I finished saying some words in Stan's honour, the church bell suddenly started to toll and as everyone was present with me in the graveyard, it seemed rather strange as to our knowledge there was nobody in the church. Maybe it was Seth giving us his final farewell!" Stan is pictured here with club member Chris Pickering at the 2004 weekend. Chris greatly respected both the man and the actor.

At this point tribute must be made to other cast members including Richard Thorp (Alan), Shirley Stelfox (Edna), Arthur Pentelow (Mr Wilks), Clive Hornby (Jack) and Kitty McGeever (Lizzie) who were all great supporters of our fan club and we wish to remember them all and feel privileged we had the chance to spend precious time with them. Emmerdale Producer, Gavin Blythe, was also an enthusiastic supporter of the club in his very successful but sadly short-lived time on the show. Jenny and the members will always remember the contribution each and every one of them made to club weekends.

Drawing of Shirley Stelfox by Paul Dacombe

Chapter 4

'Walk-On' and a trip down Memory Lane

Bryn Dennis Wilson has not only been a fan club member for many years, but has also worked on the show as a 'walk-on' or 'extra' as they used to be called in earlier times. He has lots of memories of working with the many actors and actresses from the very early days and he told us: "As a child I trained in ballet and tap-dancing and as a teenager joined an amateur dramatics association. Some years later I was given the chance to appear in Emmerdale, where I have appeared in many episodes over the years. A couple of highlights for me include being chosen to be the first person to be served a pint in the 'Woolpack' by Amos Brearley. That was a great honour and in 1993 I was involved in the spectacular plane crash scenes as an injured villager. Working alongside such stars as Richard Thorp (Alan Turner), Sheila Mercier (Annie Sugden) and also a young Ian Sharrock (Jackie Merrick) in the 1980's and 1990's brings back wonderful memories. I remember one Christmas I was having

Bryn with Richard Thorp, Plane Crash 1993

lunch with a few of the other extras and Jean Rogers (Dolly Skilbeck) brought us each a bottle of wine and said 'here you are guys have a Christmas drink on me'. What a lovely lady and it made us feel really special. The job of an extra is an important one – the 'Woolpack' would look strange without people in the background and our job is to help the artistes complete their scenes successfully and on cue.

I am very much hooked as a viewer too and I have loved the show for as long as I can remember".

Susan Hartley has special memories of her weekends in the dales: "I joined the club whilst visiting the café in Esholt where I found a leaflet advertising the fan club. I had been watching filming in the village and I signed up immediately. My first club weekend was at the Hilton Hotel in 1995 and I will always remember it fondly as it was my first. We were taken on a tour of the Tetley's Brewery and afterwards in the bar was delighted to meet 'Amos Brearley' and 'The Dingles'. Over the years I have attended many weekends and made good friends with some of the members who meet up each year. One highlight was sitting on Clive Hornby's knee for a photo at dinner – that was in the days when the cast sat with us at different tables. My favourite actor has always been Chris Chittell. He has always been very generous with his time, attending most of the club weekends. I have been very fortunate to have met so many cast members and crew as well as the production teams that make my favourite 'soap'.

Susan with Clive Hornby

I will always be grateful to Jenny and Alli for the many wonderful memories I have of the last 20 years".

Kath Jones attended her first club weekend in 1996: "My first club weekend was in 1996 at the Hilton Hotel and I remember we sang Christmas Carols at a church in Leeds. At the gala dinner on the Saturday night I was sitting next to Jane Cox (Lisa). The cast in those days sat at different tables with the fans. Jane was absolutely lovely and she could tell right away that I had a Devonshire accent. She told me her sister lived in Torquay at that time. Over the years I would see Jane at club events and she always remembered my name, which made my day.

Another weekend was at the Village Hotel in Leeds and on the Saturday evening we were entertained by the 'Woolpackers' made up of some of the cast including Steve Halliwell (Zak) Alun Lewis (Vic) and Billy Hartman (Terry). I especially remember Alison Spiro (Sarah) joining in the line dancing and we all had great fun. Another time I remember meeting Andy Devine (Shadrack) in a corridor at the hotel and he asked if we had a hairbrush he could borrow. It really made us laugh as we didn't think Shadrack ever combed his hair!

Kath with Jane Cox

Over the years I've been lucky to have made some great friends including Vanessa Thomas, Linda Loney, Ralph and Chrissie O'Flaherty, the lovely Shirley Kerrigan, Angie Stanger-Leathes and of course my best friend, Elaine Taylor, who I met in 2010 at Emmerdale.

I would like to thank Jenny and all the cast and crew for making the weekends possible for us and putting in so much effort to make everyone welcome. Hopefully there will be many more club weekends in future".

Keith and Lesley Burroughs and their son Jack are long-time members and Lesley recalls: "Having been members for a number of years (too many when I look back at how young we look in some of the early photos), I remember with fondness many of the people we've met and still meet at club gatherings. The club has given us opportunities which we would never have had otherwise; studio visits, being 'extras', meeting many cast members and being told 'behind the scenes' information from the people who make our favourite 'soap' happen. Long may the club carry on".

Keith and Lesley 20's style!

Denise Jackson has been a fan of the show for many years and attended several club weekends with her husband Neil and their young son, Ross. Denise recalls: "I dipped in and out of Emmerdale for years but became an avid fan during the 'Kathy-Dave-Kim' love triangle. I caught up on old episodes and have seen each series from the beginning.

As well as the great stories, I loved the Yorkshire scenery and on a visit to Esholt in 1999, I found a book which listed the fan club address and I joined. Through membership I have had a chance to visit private locations, the actual village and meet many members of the cast. The locations are beautiful and it is very interesting seeing behind the scenes of the show. The actors and actresses have all been lovely and generous with their time and were wonderful with my young son, Ross, who joined us on a couple of weekends. There are so many worth a mention but one that stands out is Stan Richards (Seth Armstrong). He was so charming and a true gentleman. In the show his character Seth along with Nick Bates (Cy Chadwick) displayed a plaque in memory of Archie Brooks (Tony Pitts) who died in the infamous plane crash in

Denise and Neil with Stan and Plaque

1993. The plaque was being auctioned for charity at our weekend event and my husband Neil was bidding for it as he wanted to buy it for me as a present. However he soon realised that he was bidding against Stan so he stopped bidding and Stan won the auction. Afterwards he told us he wanted to buy it as a present for Tony Pitts, so we were very pleased he was successful in the auction, despite Neil's initial efforts to win it.

The fan club is a real community and everyone is welcoming and friendly. Over the years I have made many friends and some will be life-long best friends. That's the best thing about being a member and I will always be grateful to Jenny and the fan club for that".

Neil Jackson is a gifted artist and did some paintings of the early days when the show was filmed in Arncliffe. Neil gave Tim Fee a couple as a thank-you gift for all he did to give the fans such great weekends. Imagine Neil's surprise when his one of his Arncliffe paintings was featured in a scene on the show – on the wall in Betty's living room! A surprise for Neil and Denise but also a lovely one which made them both feel very proud.

Linda Loney shared these memories: "Having watched Emmerdale since it first aired at lunchtime on 16th October 1972 (Emmerdale Farm), as a full-time mum I could watch every episode. I was delighted when I found out about the fan club in 2001, and joined as soon as I could. I then told my friend Vanessa Thomas about it and as she loved the show too, she also joined.

A painting of Arncliffe by Neil

We attended our first weekend in 2003 and straight away we met lots of people from around the world who were to become good friends – and still are to this day. I love the different dressing up themes for the gala dinners and it is amazing to see the cast make great efforts to dress up too. The photo of me here with Adam Fielding (Kirin Kotecha) shows just how much I

Linda with Adam Fielding

enjoy myself!

Since then it has been a great privilege to attend the weekends and I feel greatly honoured that we are given the opportunity to meet the cast and crew and be allowed to visit the studios and village. I would like to thank Jenny, Alli and everyone who helps our members have such great times and make precious friendships. I really hope there are many more weekends to look forward to".

It was thanks to **Vanessa Thomas** in 2003 that the club awarded an honorary membership to a lifelong fan of the show who had reached the grand old age of 99. Vanessa takes up the story: "I have been a member of the fan club since 2001 and have met some wonderful people, many of whom have become good friends. After joining the fan club I would sit and chat with my husband Stephen's grandmother about the show as I knew she had watched it from the very first episode. Grace was 97 at that time and she could remember many of the old episodes and loved talking about them. I eventually asked Jenny if she could join the club and was told she could be an honorary member. She loved receiving the newsletters from then on and as her 100th birthday approached, I thought it would be a wonderful surprise if I could arrange a birthday card signed by some of the cast for her special day. Alli Piggott organised it and Grace received a wonderful card with signed messages from the stars of the show. She also received signed cast cards too. A telegram from the Queen also made her centenary year a very special one indeed.

She passed away about 3 weeks after Stan Richards (Seth) in 2005 and she was 101. I will always remember how fondly she spoke of watching her favourite TV show. Thanks so much to Jenny, Alli and everyone connected with the fan club who made an old lady so very happy in her last few years. It is a privilege to be a member of this wonderful fan club family".

Vanessa with Charlie Hardwick

Chapter 5

A Very Special Birthday

In 1997 the show celebrated its 25th birthday and a party was held to mark the special occasion. The cast, crew and management were treated to an evening of celebration by ITV, and Jenny was invited to attend on behalf of the fan club. It was a wonderful surprise for Jenny, and also a great privilege for 4 fan club members who won a competition in the club newsletter.

Elsie Stratford was one of the winners to join in the special evening. Elsie recalls: "I have been a member since 1994 and over the years have attended club weekends where it was a wonderful opportunity to mix with the actors and actresses from the show. Many of them attend the gala dinner on the Saturday evening and they are very generous with their time and are happy to chat with the fans and have photographs taken with us.

In one of the club newsletters, I saw a competition to win a place at the coveted private party being held to celebrate 25 years of the show on our TV screens. I duly entered and was lucky enough to win a place, along with 3 other winners, Lesley Burroughs, Jenny Dutton and Margaret Cue. The party was held on 17th October 1997 at the Weetwood Hotel in Leeds. We mingled with past and present cast members and we were delighted to meet Kevin Laffan, the creator of the original 'Emmerdale Farm'. He took time to talk to everyone about those early years of the show. It was also lovely to meet such stars as Sheila Mercier (Annie), Ronald Magill (Amos), Jean Rogers (Dolly) and Frederick Pyne (Matt). The previous evening, an hour-long episode of the show was transmitted and featured Kim Tate and Steve Marchant's engagement party, which ended in tears for the Glover family.

We had a very special photo taken which shows the 4 of us with Sheila Mercier (Annie) and Stan Richards (Seth). I felt honoured and delighted to be invited with cast members to the show's 25th anniversary party".

Margaret, Jenny, Lesley and Elsie with Sheila Mercier and Stan Richards

Tottenham Cooper is another member who joined in the early days: "I joined the fan club in 1990, as soon as I heard about it. I used to go on holiday to the Yorkshire Dales every August and sometimes went to Esholt and was lucky enough to see some filming of the show. Once I watched the scenes of Eric Pollard's wedding to Elizabeth Feldman when her son was arrested for robbery outside Home Farm. It was great to see such screen characters as Seth, Amos and Mr Wilks and one day I met Richard Thorp and his Harley Davidson motorbike, which he loved very much.

The first club weekend I attended was in 1997 at the Village Hotel in Leeds. Everyone was friendly and welcoming and I met two new friends, Ken Bryant and Glen Mason, and we attended many club events for quite a few years, often bidding successfully to win studio and village trips. The first weekend I won a day at the studios and watched some filming. I even got to do a scene in the Post Office with Chris Chittell (Eric), Alun Lewis and Deena Payne (Vic and Viv) and they all made me feel very

Tottenham (centre) with Ken and Glen

welcome. We haven't been able to attend for the last few years but I still keep in touch with Ken and Glen and we meet up once or twice a year in Bristol or Bath and enjoy talking about our happy days in the dales. I did attend this year in 2016 and saw many old friends and familiar faces. It was absolutely fantastic to see everyone again and enjoy the company of the cast and crew for much of the weekend.

In 1999 I did the Coast to Coast walk from St Bees Head to Robin Hood's Bay – a total of 192 miles. I managed to raise £700 for St James' Hospital in Leeds and the Chairman of the charity turned up at the club hotel on the Saturday to accept my cheque.

Joining the fan club has been one of the best things I have ever done. I've met so many wonderful people and I would like to give my congratulations to Jenny for being such a great club leader and thanks to the cast and crew who have given their time so generously over many years for club members".

Peter Sanguine is the club's longest serving overseas member since 1992. Peter lives in New Zealand so has not been able to attend club weekends, but did manage to visit Esholt on a trip to the UK to visit family: "I became a member of the Emmerdale Club after watching several episodes of 'Emmerdale Farm' during my visit to England in 1992. The sheer joy and pleasure I got from watching the show certainly had an impact on me and I felt compelled to join the club. I really enjoy being a member and look forward to the newsletters which are full of interesting information. The events for the members give them the opportunity to meet each other and portrays a sense of camaraderie and belonging to a family of like-minded people who love Emmerdale. The show is in my blood, the acting is very professional with story-lines that reflect issues of everyday life. The beautiful Yorkshire country scenes shown in the programme are a real bonus. I dearly hope that one day I will be able to attend a club event.

On my 1992 visit, I went with my family to Esholt and then we attended a car-washing fundraiser event where I was lucky enough to meet Chris Chittell (Eric). I told him I was a fan from New Zealand and he made me feel very welcome and it was a privilege to meet one of the show's great characters.

I have also been amazed to read about the growth of the overseas membership of the fan club. Jenny must be congratulated for her great work at the helm, and I am also delighted that Sir Peter Leitch, who is very well known in New Zealand, is also an honorary member.

Finally, both Emmerdale and the club are very special to me and it is fantastic to belong to such a wonderful family. Best wishes and good fortune to Jenny for the next 25 years, long may it continue and thanks to fellow fans for making our club such a success for everyone".

Peter with Chris Chittell

Kaarina Suvanto from Finland attended her first weekend in 2000, having joined the club the previous year: "I was delighted to be selected to attend the 10th club anniversary weekend at the Weetwood Hotel in January 2000. I had the idea that most of the members would be older people – how wrong I was! The first member I met was Tottenham Cooper and during that first weekend I managed to speak to around 70 of the 120 members present. Some of them were interested to find out how Emmerdale was doing in Finland. As a translator, I could have done with a photographer but had to make do with taking as many photos as possible myself, in case it was the only weekend I would be able to attend.

Kaarina and Emmerdale sign

On the Saturday evening I was delighted to meet cast members including Lisa Riley, James Hooton, and Claire King. I noticed that older fans always referred to the cast using their real names so I tried to do the same but I didn't know all of them. It was a pity I met Sheree Murphy who played Tricia Dingle only after I had taken my camera back to my room. She was excited about her recent visit to Lapland in Finland and I must say I have seldom seen such a radiant smile – what a charming lady she was. All in all every cast member was very friendly and seemed to really appreciate the fans.

The following year I started up the Finnish fan club with Minna Valkealahti with the help of Jenny and Tim Fee. It was lovely to attend future weekends with new Finnish members and meet new cast and club members every year.

What I have always found most interesting are the talks by members of the crew telling us all about their work behind the scenes – how lovely of them to share it with the members and they show such devotion to their work.

After retiring from running the Finnish club I missed some weekends but was delighted to attend the 25th anniversary weekend which was held in March 2016. It was absolutely wonderful to see so many familiar faces and to thank Jenny for all of her hard work. May there be many more years to celebrate!"

Jean and Terry Reason joined the club in 1997 and recall: "Whilst on holiday in York we decided to visit Ripley Castle. When we arrived we saw a notice advertising a cricket match between teams from 'Emmerdale' and 'The Bill'. Ripley Castle was left for another day as we had no intention of missing the cricket match!

Whilst there we were delighted to find out about the Emmerdale fan club and as soon as we returned home we both joined as we love the show. We have thoroughly enjoyed being members and Jenny does an excellent job of running the club. We very much look forward to attending the special weekends each year. Emmerdale has a very happy and friendly cast and crew which makes for a lovely atmosphere, and they are willing to give up their time to make the weekends so enjoyable for us. Well done Jenny and long may the club continue".

Terry and Jean Reason in the village

Linda Beatty recalls: "I joined the club in 1997. I had started watching the show when it was Emmerdale Farm in 1974 and it was broadcast in the early afternoons. I have watched re-runs of earlier episodes so have probably seen most of them.

Unknown to me, my husband Michael bid in an auction run by the 'Sun' newspaper to raise funds for an earthquake appeal and I became the proud owner of 'Charity's' wedding dress! It was the dress she wore for her proposed marriage to Tom King in 2005, which did not go ahead as she was jilted at the altar. Sadie King had produced some photos of Charity kissing Cain which was a set up as Sadie feared she would lose her inheritance to Charity. I was delighted when Michael surprised me with the dress. It is a beautiful garment, signed by Charity (Emma Atkins) and even has some good old Emmerdale dirt on it as there was a fight between the Dingles and the Kings and Charity was pushed to the ground!

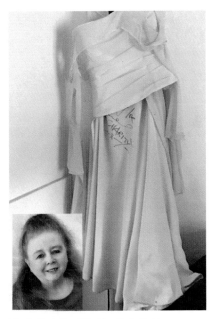

Linda (inset) with Charity's Dress

Well done Jenny and the fan club – and thanks to everyone who makes our club so special".

Chapter 6

A Right Royal Decade

The dawn of the new decade in January 2000 saw the fan club celebrate its 10th anniversary, and 2002 produced one of the proudest days in the fictional village – the visit of Queen Elizabeth II, in the year of her Golden Jubilee. The purpose built village of Emmerdale was built on land owned by the Queen's cousin, Lord Harewood, and it was a great honour for ITV when the visit was confirmed. The show's Line Producer, Tim Fee, made arrangements for the visit and there was collective relief when the Queen's Rolls Royce managed to make its way over the narrow bridge to Main Street. Tim had even arranged for special effects co-ordinator, Ian Rowley, to blow up the Post Office especially for the visit! Happily it all went according

Tim Fee in the Woolpack

to plan and the Queen took it all in her royal stride. It was very special for the management, cast and crew to meet the Queen in her Jubilee year which also saw the show celebrate 30 years on TV – a marvellous achievement for ITV.

Tim Fee was affectionately known as 'The Mayor of Emmerdale' and he joined the staff in 1988 until his retirement in 2009. Tim was always very committed to the fan club and helped plan many weekends during his years on the show. Although retired, Tim was more than happy to share some memories. Over to you Tim!

"Gosh, it doesn't seem like more than 25 years since I visited London Zoo for the first time ever along with Ronnie Magill (Amos Brearley), Arthur Pentelow (Mr Wilks), Stan Richards (Seth Armstrong), Cy Chadwick (Nick Bates), Glenda McKay (Rachel Hughes) and a lady who I didn't really know called Jenny Godfrey, who had come up with the idea of forming a club for fans of Emmerdale. I must say at that stage I hadn't a clue how it would take off but observing Jenny's total conviction and dedication, I thought 'well let's give it a go'. Little did I know how successful and loyal this club was going to

Tim Fee and Prue Haynes on 'weekend' duty

be! As time went on Jenny and I chatted about how we could do something more special for our loyal friends than just send them a newsletter so we came up with the idea of a weekend, devoted totally to the club giving access that no other organisation would ever give. But had I really thought this through? How was I going to entertain 150 people from Friday to Sunday at the Weetwood Hotel in Leeds with all things Emmerdale and whom would I get to help as the crew worked so hard during the week putting in extremely long hours just to make the show. But I need not have worried.

As always, key members of my staff stepped forward and offered to be a part of the team and most of them stayed with me throughout my time with the club. Alli Piggott and her husband Don, Val and Prue and of course for our older members, who could forget the enigmatic Roly, who seemed to turn up around every corner! Of course there were many other people who assisted over the years and without their valuable support, none of the fun could have happened.

So what memories do I have of those great weekends? … here's a few that might jog the memory if you were present. I always remember our Friday evening welcome at the Weetwood Hotel which very quickly became an international event with the presence of our friends from Finland. Then the first opportunity to meet up with some members of cast who came along to meet and sign autographs. Dinner and a quiz followed and an opportunity to watch that evening's episode then hopefully an early night before the mad rush of Saturday's hectic schedule.

Tours of the Emmerdale studios in small groups would start the day and I can clearly remember taking one group through the doors of the studio at Burley Road when a great roaring sound was heard in the sky and what should fly over our heads but Concorde en route for the airport … of course I had laid it on specially!

Club members would get so excited with their cameras (pre digital days) and were very soon running out of film, but who should appear seemingly out of nowhere just at the right moment but Roly Plant, with rolls of film to save the day! After visiting the studios we would visit the Prop stores and then on to 'The Works', the graphic company who provided lots of printed and photographic material for the show. Amazingly they would provide a calendar by the following day with a picture of the whole weekend group, usually taken outside Home Farm.

We would then move on for a real location lunch exactly as the cast and crew eat during the week, cooked by our location caterers and eaten in style on the dining buses!

The afternoon would be taken up with various visits and talks given by staff from different departments but most noticeably by our special effects expert Ian Rowley who would proudly show us around his workshop often wheeling out Dusty Bin! But how many of you remember the infamous Saturday when a raffle was held with the winner getting the opportunity to shoot me? Yes, I think you can still find it on YouTube under 'Who Shot Tim Fee'!

Saturday evening was always the big gala dinner with the infamous charity auctions and raffles and lots of the stars to meet, chat to and dance the night away. The following morning would see us all dashing off once again (no time for hangovers) to walk around Emmerdale village and try and piece together the clues left in various places by Mike Long (the man responsible for designing and building the village).

Then it was back to the Weetwood for a warming Sunday Lunch with the final auction, which always seemed to be won by the 3 musketeers Ken, Glen and Tottenham, (for those of you who can remember them). Then sad goodbyes and a date in the diary for the following year to do it all over again.

The weekend format never really changed, but then nobody wanted it to. There was always fantastic support from the cast and crew of the show, many of whom attended at some point over the weekend.

But what memories do I have of special events that happened during my time? One particular highlight I clearly remember was a special Christmas Carol service held at Leeds Parish Church with Carols and Christmas readings from the cast.

Do you remember attending the cricket matches at Ripley, a private marquee for club members, when the first prize in the raffle was to blow up Seth's shed? Or even to fire Eric Pollard from the mouth of a cannon like a human cannonball? One year we even had our very own private fly past of the Red Arrows!

Oh so many happy memories and the weekend still continues which is all down to the hard work of the very dedicated Jenny Godfrey and of course the Emmerdale team, without whom none of this would ever happen.

I remember it all with great fondness. Good Luck 'Emmerdale Club' and long may it continue".

The royal theme continued during the decade with the introduction of the aptly named 'King' family in 2004. Only one of the original family members, Jimmy King (Nick Miles) has survived through to 2016. The head of the family, Tom King, was murdered on Christmas Day, 2006 and Carl King (Tom Lister) famously met his death in the 'live' episode filmed in 2012, the anniversary of the show's 40th birthday.

Kath Beedles was appointed Series Producer of Emmerdale in 2005 having worked on the show since 2001. Kath was responsible for many major storylines including 'Who Killed Tom King?' which was nominated for best storyline at the British Soap Awards in 2007. Kath has written some words in tribute to the show and the fan club: "I spent a formative part of my career working at Emmerdale and have now worked on all the British 'soaps'. I can say with authority that Emmerdale's fan club and its weekends are very special and utterly unique. This fantastic club, like Emmerdale itself, has a warmth and family feel I've not experienced elsewhere.

Kath Beedles

'Emmerdalians' (as 'Hoodlum' coined Emmerdale fans during the 'Who Killed Tom King?' channel they created with us) are a rare breed of soap fans – loyal, passionate, welcoming, generous, informed and a right good laugh. At a weekend evening event a drink is always in hand, the dance floor is never empty and no raffle prize goes unsold.

When I think of fan club weekends, I think of the Weetwood Hotel, of lovely conversations with fans, great food and a long night in the bar. When I became Series Producer and there were worries when we'd told a controversial story – would anyone challenge me about it? – an Emmerdalian is forthright in their opinions, but any critical feedback came with warmth and understanding so my nerves were unwarranted. And of course when I think of the fan club and its weekends, I think of two people without whom I can't imagine them existing – Jenny and Tim. They made the club weekends a riot yet seamless and smooth running – it's no mean feat to pull together such a varied calendar with so many people, without a hitch. To this day Jenny and the current team keep it running as smoothly as ever.

As I sit here to write this, I'm smiling and flooded with good feelings at the memories. The television industry isn't always a welcoming place to be, but the Emmerdale fan club is an oasis within it.

Congratulations on your 25th anniversary. Thank you for the memories and good times".

Prue Haynes worked at Emmerdale for many of her 40 years with ITV and during the tenures of both Tim and Kath. Stage Manager Prue recalls: "I loved being involved with the fan club. From humble beginnings Tim Fee made them such fun and Jenny, the fan club founder, was so calm in sorting out any queries. As time went on, they became 'packed' weekends with things going on all of the time. First it was at the studios at Sunny Bank Mills then at 27, Burley Road and nowadays you see the sets in the main building.

Getting you into all the coaches and gathering you up at the village was a challenge sometimes. The crew often had the quest of finding some of you in obscure places!

Why did it always seem to rain or snow on our trips to the village? I know we had a few years of decent weather but mostly I remember dressing in my wet-weather gear to combat the lashing wind and ice on the ground. But that didn't deter your enjoyment of participating in the village competitions compiled by Mike Long and latterly Robert Scott.

Weekend quizzes were the norm and I was happy to take over the marking duties from Jenny, especially when Tim discovered she was working well into the Saturday night/Sunday morning to get it finished.

I know I was bossy when getting (or perhaps herding!) you all on to the buses but that's 'The Commander' for you. Sometimes it wasn't the fans I had to sort out. A trip to Home Farm comes to mind when I had to instruct the driver of a rather large lorry to move it to give our bus room to pass and carry on our journey up a narrow hill. What the bus driver thought I have no idea but we made it safely back to the hotel, which was the object of the operation.

You, the fans, are what make the weekends special. It was always good to see you and catch up on your news and have a good chin-wag. Seeing children grow from being babies into adulthood is a lasting memory for me. You have all been so loyal and long may it last. Since retiring I have not attended but want to congratulate Jenny. May the fan club have many more weekends in the future".

Chapter 7

Kindly Leave the Set Please!

Fan club members are privileged and trusted 'on set' when they visit the studios and the village on club weekends. Many of the crew generously give their time to help make the club weekends so very special for the fans and every club member is well aware that every respect must be given to the working environments of the ITV staff. The cast and crew featured here will be very familiar to members so let's take a peek behind the scenes and see who we can find to share some fan club memories:

Emmerdale cast and crew at fan club weekend 2014

Chris Chittell: "I do not know who it was that suggested forming such a club, unheard of in any other likeminded 'circles'!

However the members, every last one of them, are, and have been for the last 25 years, our extended family. What also is very much in evidence is the way everyone looks out for one another – charming! A joy to see you all – including the 'terrible twins'!"

Gaynor Faye: "The Emmerdale fan weekend is a chance for us to meet and thank our wonderful, loyal supporters. The show wouldn't be the success it is without them. I hope they rejoice in the recent accolades as much as we all do, knowing they've helped to achieve Emmerdale's huge success. From the bottom of my heart a big thank you to the fan club members".

Patrick Mower: "I was fortunate to have a fan club of my own in my 'Callan' and 'Special Branch' days so I know how hard it is to keep the support system going! None of us at Emmerdale take our popularity for granted and we really appreciate the loyalty, the affection and indeed the love that the Emmerdale fan club have for the show. Thank you all for your support over the last 25 years".

Laura Norton: "Congratulations to Jenny and the fan club members on reaching 25 years – what a milestone! The unconditional support from the fans year upon year is utterly heartwarming. We wouldn't have a show without you. Big love, Laura".

Danny Miller: "I love the Emmerdale fan club, particularly the annual weekends they host where the cast can sit down and chat with some of this fantastic show's true and dedicated fans. I have met some of the most enthusiastic and genuine people at these events, and will continue to support Jenny and Angie and the rest of the team for their devotion to the show and this fan club in particular. Hope to see you all on the next one!"

Liam Fox: "25 years of the Emmerdale fan club – what an amazing achievement. I know myself and the cast really enjoy catching up with lots of fans every year at the club weekends – brilliant!"

John Bowe: "One of the great pleasures of being involved in a show like Emmerdale is the contact with the fans. Their devotion and dedication to Emmerdale is astonishing. The fan club gives us all a chance to meet those fans and they are always so supportive".

Mike Parr: "The fan club is an amazing way to meet some of the fans that I've had contact with online. It's nice to be able to thank the fans personally when I meet them at club weekends. The fans are just as important as we are. It's a fun weekend where everyone gets together and we all have a great time".

Bhasker Patel: "The fan club weekends are fun filled and we spend time celebrating with die-hard fans who come from all over the UK and abroad".

Bill Ward: "Congratulations to the Emmerdale fan club celebrating 25 great years. Thanks for all the tremendous support you give the show. Wishing you many, many more years of fan club memories".

Charlie Hardwick is no longer in the show but has very fond memories of the fan club weekends: "For a fan club to celebrate 25 years is an incredible achievement which wouldn't be possible without so many dedicated fans. I've met some lovely people over the years at the vibrant and unique club weekends which made me feel a much deeper connection with our audience. Cheers everyone!"

Alli Piggott: "It's amazing to think that the Emmerdale fan club is now into its 26th year – so many happy memories and so many wonderful people.

I am enormously proud to be involved with the whole event and during the last few years since our 'Mayor of Emmerdale' (Tim Fee) retired, I have taken on more of an organisational role which has meant a lot more involvement in the planning stages, and of course a total 'hands on' approach with the weekend event itself, together with much guidance and help from Matt Cleary, the Head of Production.

The Emmerdale fan club weekend simply could not take place each year without the commitment and dedication of the brilliant team of crew volunteers around me. This group of people (too many to mention by name) and not forgetting my husband, Don Piggott, all give up their time each year for the entire weekend to assist with everything and anything that is required in order to make the event a success.

All of the team are tremendously proud of the show, the sets, the village locations etc and it really is everyone's passion that carries it forward. We all particularly look forward to meeting up with fan club members, old and new, and always welcome feedback and new ideas from the fans as to how they perceive the weekend as a whole. After all the main aim of the weekend is for everyone to have fun!

Don and Alli Piggott enjoying the weekend

We have gradually been bringing in changes to the original format; not an easy task to come up with new and fresh ideas (one of the major changes was to look at slowing down the pace of the weekend) to allow more flexibility and relaxation time for everyone, including not such an early start to the Saturday and Sunday mornings!

We are always looking at ways to keep the weekend exciting and varied and have adopted a theme each year for the Saturday night gala dinner which has been great fun. Themes including Hollywood and Halloween have been very popular, and all supported by live bands (some including cast members) and disco sounds after dinner.

We know how much the fans enjoy the interaction with the cast and this year we included the opportunity for members to act out a scene with cast in the Woolpack, under direction, with cameras rolling exactly as we do for real scenes. The fans responded brilliantly and you could feel the excitement on set and we received great feedback from everyone.

Organised workshops with various departments is another new favourite, allowing members a close-up of how the show really works including make-up, costumes, props, directors, sound, cameras etc. We have tried to include as much as possible to give the fans a varied and interesting itinerary.

Sunday and the final lunch comes around all too quickly for everyone and after the goodbyes it really is time for myself and the team to unwind … and begin planning for next year!"

Val Lawson: "When I joined Yorkshire Television in June 1973, it was definitely a 'man's world'. The Assistant Directors' department of today was known then as Unit Managers and Call Boys (the Call Boy title originated from the theatre). It took me some time but eventually I changed the company's mind about only using men and became the first female 'Call Boy' and then on to becoming a Unit Manager. Today the job titles have changed and our department is now made up of 1st, 2nd and 3rd Assistant Directors.

Val Lawson in Emmerdale village

Over the years I have worked on many different types of programmes – dramas, entertainment, sit-coms, children's, sport, religion and of course 'Emmerdale Farm'. In the early days we transmitted 2 episodes a week with the wonderful Amos, Mr Wilks, Annie, Grandad, Jack, Joe, Matt, Dolly, Seth etc.

Today, at ITV's Leeds studios, we now exclusively make Emmerdale. Transmitting 6 episodes per week and with a larger number of cast members, we needed to increase our department. On average, we have 3 teams recording 12 episodes every two weeks. As the 1st Assistant Director I create the 'Call Sheet' for my team – this document includes all of the information required for the 'Shoot' – the location and studio shooting schedule, call times for cast and crew, equipment and so on. On the recording days the 1st A.D. is in charge of the shoot, co-ordinating all of the various departments and making sure that we complete that day's schedule. As I mentioned we have 3 teams, all shooting at the same time – this becomes tricky as we have only one group of actors and one of each 'set'. Each cast member can be moving from one team to another throughout the day and recording any number of scenes from the 12 episodes!

We all really love working on Emmerdale and are very proud that we are the only 'soap' with an official fan club, created of course by the brilliant Jenny Godfrey. Jenny is amazing and I am so pleased that she came into our lives. Over the years I have attended most of the fan club weekends and have made many friends along the way. It's also wonderful to see friends arriving from so far afield as Finland, Sweden, Ireland and the USA. I love it when there are Emmerdale charity events and we meet up with so many of the club members who are there to support us.

I may only see some of the Emmerdale family once a year but it feels like no time at all since we all met up. We've all 'grown up' together and I love it when I'm given a photo of me from years ago – was I ever that young?? Over the years the photographs do create some wonderful memories, reminding us of the hundreds of actors and actresses who have attended the weekends. We also share sad memories of lost members of cast and friends over the years. How lucky we are to have Jenny and the fan club and be able to share such special moments together. The club weekends have evolved over the years and more of the production crew are with us – now creating budding actors out of some of the club members!

I feel very proud and privileged to be part of the Emmerdale family – the cast, crew, production team and fan club – we all have a part to play.

Thank you dear Jenny for all your hard work and dedication; you are an extraordinary lady. When you created the fan club you opened up the world for so many people to share and be a part of Emmerdale. You are very special and I thank you for letting me be a part of it".

Dave Cowan works in the Props and Buying departments: "When I joined Emmerdale I thought it would be just another job, nothing special, same old, same old. How wrong I was; it didn't take me long to discover I was part of something very special, very special indeed. I had joined a family, a great team and a top show.

Then to find out we had a fan club, no other 'soap' had anything like it. We are so fortunate to have a superb club with such a vibrant membership, a club which is still going strong after 25 years.

This is all due to the efforts and dedication of Jenny. A real lady with a passion second to none for Emmerdale. She has worked so very hard to keep our fan club going over the years. Thank you Jenny for all you have done and continue to do for our fans and our show.

I made up my mind to do as much as possible for the club and the many dedicated and loyal fans. As a member of the Emmerdale team, I feel it is only right to give something back to our fans. The bottom line is without the fans and

Dave Cowan and splendid kilt at Aberdeen event

their love of the show, there would be no show and I wouldn't be in the best job anyone could wish for. After working at the studios for a while, I was lucky enough to be taken onto the fan club crew, headed by the wonderful Alli Piggott. She has been a real inspiration for me and through her support, I hopefully have given the fans and the club good service and helped to make them feel special.

Between us we have seen many changes to the show over the years and the vast majority have been good. Many, many great and challenging storylines, and many more to come. We have progressed from transmitting a couple of episodes a week, now up to 5 days a week, one of which being a double episode. Now we are all recognised as being the best 'soap' on TV and rightly so. We all know Emmerdale is the best.

It still amazes me after all these years how we still produce a strong and vibrant show. Every day when I pass through the gates into studio I feel proud to be part of it all. Proud to be part of such a hard-working and dedicated team and proud of our hardcore of fans. It all comes together to make the greatest 'soap' on television .... EMMERDALE".

Adam Sales: "I always love being a part of the fan club weekend. It's so important for us to connect with our audience in this way. Their passion for the show is infectious. They are more than just fans – they are friends of the show and we've had so much fun together over the years".

Amy Ormsby: "Fan club weekends are always lots of fun to be part of. It's so nice to catch up with some familiar faces and also meet new members who have never experienced the club weekend. The team loves coming up with fresh, new and exciting ways of

Adam Sales and Dusty Bin!

showing off the sets and the beautiful village location. My favourite part is the gala dinner on the Saturday evening where you can get dressed up, have a giggle and a good old boogie on the dance floor!"

Anna Coleman: "I've really enjoyed helping out with the fan club event as part of the decorating committee for the last two years. I love how we start off with a bin bag of decorations and by the end of the day Weetwood Hall is transformed back in time to reflect a previous decade, or into a Hollywood-style venue. This is made even more authentic by the effort everyone makes with their outfits, and it's a great way of bringing everyone together to celebrate Emmerdale once a year".

Tribute must be made here on behalf of all the fan club members who have attended club weekends over the years – heartfelt thanks to the cast and crew who have given their time and dedication to make the weekends so very special. Your efforts are truly appreciated.

Chapter 8

Fans from Home and Abroad

John Keppy joined the fan club in 2003 and with a long-standing interest in the performing arts, was delighted to meet the actors and actresses as well as making friends with many like-minded fans of the show: "Since joining the club it has always been a joy to meet up with friends old and new on a yearly basis at the club weekends. I look forward to every visit and over the years have had very interesting discussions with crew members such as Dave Cowan, Prue Haynes, Val Lawson, Adam Sales and Kate Oates who have all been happy to spend time chatting about their various roles within the production team. Of course there have been many actors to talk to and admire, and some who have especially impressed me over the years are Chris Chittell (Eric), Deena Payne (Viv), Danny Miller (Aaron) and Kelvin Fletcher (Andy). I also think Charley Webb (Debbie) is one of those rare breed who have evolved from childhood into an amazing dramatic actress as an adult. It has always been special to me to spend time

John and Charley Webb

socialising with some of the cast too and my favourite drinking partners are Bhasker Patel and Matthew Wolfenden. They show such dedication and friendliness to the club members, it really is a thrill to be in their company.

Jayne with Charlie Hardwick

The fan club would be nothing without the huge input from Alli Piggott and her wonderful team of helpers from the production team. Also Tim Fee must be mentioned here as he was devoted to our club for many years until his retirement.

Finally, the biggest thank you of all must go to Jenny Godfrey who runs the club, organises us all at Emmerdale events and is just a thoroughly lovely lady - bless you Jenny xxx"

Jayne Shanahan is currently the only fan club member from the United States. Following 25 years working in the Florida court system she retired to Ireland in 2003. Jayne takes up the story: "In 2005 I turned on my television and was pleasantly surprised to recognise Mark Charnock on screen. I had loved watching him in the

Bhasker Patel with Jayne's painting

BBC series 'Cadfael' so this discovery led to watching Emmerdale and my devotion to the show began from there. A few years later I discovered a new Irish friend, Sheila McGrath, had been a big fan of the show for more than 25 years. Sheila told me about the fan club and I noticed in one of her newsletters there was mention of a club weekend. Sheila had not applied previously as she had no-one to travel with so without delay we applied to go on the next weekend in 2010. Since then there has been no stopping us and thanks to Jenny's kindness we have been regulars ever since and also enjoy the lunches in London too.

When I retired to Ireland it gave me the opportunity and time to resume a great hobby of mine, painting. Inspired by a fellow fan, Birthe from Sweden, I started painting scenes from Emmerdale village and presenting them to Alli Piggott to auction for charity at the gala dinners. I am very proud to say that Chris Chittell owns my painting of the infamous village bus stop. At the 25th anniversary weekend in 2016, fan club regular John Keppy bought what I believe to be my best painting to date of the 'Woolpack'. Alli did tell me that Matt Cleary was sorry to have missed out in the bidding as he was going to display it in the actual 'Woolpack' itself. It made me feel very proud.

Jenny's brilliant creation, the 'Emmerdale fan club' has been a source of great enjoyment and inspiration. Wonderful friendships have been forged during the last 6 years or so. Meeting Mark Charnock (Marlon) each year has been a real joy and all of the cast members and production staff are gracious and welcoming. Here's to another 25 years of the fan club!"

Arja Pullinen has been a fan of the show for many years, watching it from her home in Finland: "I've been watching Emmerdale on Finnish TV for more than 15 years now. I've always liked the English language and English TV shows. Right from the start I was hooked – I love the scenery, the normal looking people and the language.

Arja at Home Farm

I never thought I could get so much involved, but there was no turning back after joining the Finnish Emmerdale club in 2002. I joined the English club a few years later.

Finland is approximately two years behind with story-lines, but the most enthusiastic of us, me included, watch the current episodes on the internet which means we are up to date with the latest stories in the dales.

My first two weekends were in 2004 and 2005 and then again from 2010 onwards. Each time has been in a way better than the previous one. You get to know people more, make new friends and meet new members of the cast. There are always new places to find in the village and new settings in the studios and you generally know your way around much better.

During these last few years I have made many new friends from England, Ireland and Sweden. We have so much fun and I also try to attend club lunches when possible. I really appreciate the friendships I have made.

I've also met some of the cast in their theatre performances in London, which has also been great fun. My friend and fellow member, Jacky Steers, joined me at the King's Head Theatre, where we met Matt Healy who was appearing in 'The Murder Game'. We also met up with Nick Miles when he was in 'Meeting Joe Strummer'. In the Summer of 2014 Jacky and I went to see Karl Davies in Regent Park's open air theatre. It has been great fun meeting up with them and chatting to them after performances.

To summarise : Emmerdale and the fan club have given me more than I can describe, feelings from sorrow to anger or even fear, to happiness to joy and even giggling aloud when watching some scenes between Nicola and Jimmy. I also have had the opportunity to be part of the Emmerdale family during the special weekends, and find many lovely, new friends.

The show also owes me one hour of breathing; I forgot to do that when I watched the last two episodes where Cameron's life came to an end!

I can't thank Jenny Godfrey, ITV's Matt Cleary and Alli Piggott enough for organising such fantastic events for the fans to take part in and enjoy. Thank you everyone".

Geoff Dixon has been a member for almost 16 years: "I was born in Leeds and work as a supervisor at Headingly Cricket Club, where I have met such famous people as Dickie Bird and Sir Geoffrey Boycott. I also love watching Emmerdale and I get to meet even more famous actors and actresses from the show. Although I live just 15 minutes from the Weetwood Hotel in Leeds, I still attend the full club weekend. As soon as I walk through the hotel doors I forget I am from Leeds until Sunday afternoon when we all say our farewells.

Geoff with Malandra Burrows

I've made some wonderful friends over the years and we all look forward to meeting up for the weekends and club lunches. Special friends include Norman Cooper, June Brown, Jenny Dutton, Susan Hartley and Steve Marshall. I must also mention Angie Stanger-Leathes who is lovely and has written this book. She is the only reason why I watch Newcastle United! There are lots of other great fans too who I have met during my time as a member.

I also want to thank Jenny Godfrey who started it all and the cast and crew of Emmerdale who work so hard to make it a fantastic experience for the fans".

James Lynes joined the club in 2003 : "My first memory of the club is being aged 15 and I was reading 'Inside Soap' when I found information about how to join. In 2003 I sent off my application and when I received the first newsletter I saw that they were planning their next Emmerdale fan weekend.

I knew straight away I had to go! I was lucky to get a place and on 23th January 2004 aged 16, I travelled from my home in Cornwall to Leeds. I had to change trains four times but made it eventually. That evening at the hotel I was nervous and excited as I met Patrick Mower, Shirley Stelfox and Dominic Brunt.

James with Shirley Stelfox

That first weekend was amazing and despite problems with my sight, I befriended many fellow fans including two guide dogs who belonged to Rowan and Glenn Graham. I was looked after very well by Don and Alli Piggott, Roly Plant, Val Lawson and Prue Haynes. The Emmerdale staff could not do enough for me and were so kind and made sure all went went for me. Another highlight was meeting the actor Richard Moore who played Jarvis. He lived in Cornwall and offered me a lift home but I wanted to visit the Emmerdale sets so I had to turn him down, but it was a wonderful gesture.

Amos in the snow

Fast forward 6 years and I had attended every year since 2003. People who know me will remember I used a white cane in those days due to my sight difficulties. I later applied for a guide dog and I was offered a labrador and he was called Amos. I could hardly believe it and it made me think straight away of Amos and Mr Wilks behind the bar in the Woolpack! Amos travelled with me for a few years to the weekends and was a great favourite with the cast and fellow members. Sadly he passed away in 2015 but I have wonderful memories of him and our times together.

I've met some wonderful actors and actresses over the years and my favourite being Lorraine Chase who would always give me a kiss on the cheek! Other special cast members for me are Patrick Mower, Shirley Stelfox, Richard Thorp, Stan Richards, Jane Cox and Mark Charnock. My dream is to meet Malandra Burrows but she left Emmerdale before I had the chance to meet her so don't think it will ever happen now.

Thank you Jenny and the cast and crew at Emmerdale. Thank you for making my dreams come true. I wish the club many more happy years".

Chapter 9

Another Milestone and Love is in the Air!

In 2010, the fan club reached its 20th anniversary and as always on significant dates, Matt Cleary and his crew provided a fantastic celebration for the fans. In February 2010 when the packed coaches arrived in the village, there was a very special ceremony awaiting everyone. Jenny, along with Alli Piggott and Val Lawson, helped to plant a magnolia bush in the garden of Mill Cottage, to mark the club's 20 wonderful years. The bush is still flourishing for all to see and enjoy in 2016 and many of us were pleased to see it doing so well, 6 years after it was planted.

Sally and Lisa with Liam and Aaron

Sally Gaden and Lisa Woodland were two of the fans that year – their friendship blossomed after meeting through their mutual love of the show. They are pleased to share their stories with us:

Sally Gaden: "If it wasn't for Emmerdale, my life would have been so different in so many ways. It's been a massive part of my life since 1991 when, after my Nana passed away, I continued in her tradition of watching every episode. When I joined the club, also in 1991, I didn't realise what a huge change this would mean to my life and that I was subscribing into such a friendly and happy family group of fans. My first club memory was from 1992 when a small group of us met with Jenny at Farsley Mill for a tour of the studio and we had lunch with a few of the cast members. I was hooked! From there it grew and grew, attending cricket matches and travelling to see the cast in various stage shows.

The birth of the internet changed things dramatically when I became a member of a fan message-board in 2003 which was set up by fellow member, Jacky Steers. I started to chat to a member called 'Moggysgirl' and little did I know what this initial contact would lead to! We exchanged messages daily and arranged to meet in Leeds, three years later in 2006. The rest is private history and Lisa and I have now celebrated 10 years together.

I must thank Emmerdale for bringing Lisa and her two sons into my life, and for the past 25 years of fun and enjoyment, supporting and following this wonderful Yorkshire soap".

Lisa Woodland: "It is so difficult to put into words just how special Emmerdale and the fan club are to me, as I have so much history to cover. I first fell in love with the show back in 1989 when I was 10 years old. Claire King (Kim Tate) had already joined the show and she became my favourite cast member and from that moment I could never miss an episode!

I wasn't aware there was a fan club but as soon as I found out about it I badgered my dad constantly to let me join and eventually we both became members. He would take me all over the country to meet the cast at various events such as the cricket matches, which were amazing in those days as the fan club had its own special tent where you could meet the cast and crew. We would also go to watch some of the actors in stage shows and to show our support for all things Emmerdale! One of our favourite experiences thanks to the club, was becoming 'extras' for the filming at the Tate's Heritage Farm in 1994. I'll never forget watching Seth with a ferret down his trousers and being able to watch the cast actually filming was a dream come true for me.

Not only have I grown up with the show and the club, so have both of my children, Liam and Aaron, who from being very small have attended so many events and shows. Aaron in particular loves meeting the cast and crew and being a part of the fan club. I have met some lovely people over the years and some have become wonderful friends to me and my family. Also through our joint love for the show and the club, I met my partner Sally and we have now celebrated 10 amazing years together. That is why the club and the show will forever hold such a special place in my heart. It has brought people together in such a wonderful way and I feel lucky to be part of such a fabulous community".

Lisa's youngest son Aaron is 14 years old and wants to share these memories:

Aaron Woodland: "My mum has always been a massive fan of Emmerdale, so right from being a baby in a pushchair me and my brother Liam went to events such as cricket and football with her even though I can't remember meeting actors such as Patrick Mower, Frazer Hines and Chris Chittell back then, as I was too young to remember them.

My first memory was when I was 5 and I went to a charity football match as I love the game. I met Luke Tittensor and Glen Lamont and enjoyed

Aaron - happy as a kid in a sweetshop!

watching the match. I wanted to go to more events and at a cricket match

I met Charley Webb and Matthew Wolfenden, who are my favourites. At each event I met more cast members and enjoyed adding photographs and autographs to my collection.

My mum asked me if I would like to join the fan club and I was really pleased. My first weekend was in 2012 and dancing with Michelle Hardwick was one of my best memories and when Laura Norton called me 'the cutest Emmerdale fan ever' it was awesome. I've got to know some of the crew members too and I really like Rachel and Ruth and Dave from Props has always been lots of fun. When I received a huge teddy bear from ITV to thank me for being a big fan it was fantastic so thanks to Matt Cleary for organising it.

One of my favourite events was at Aberdeen when we stayed in the same hotel as the cast and I remember arm-wrestling with Matthew Wolfenden and play-fighting with Michael Parr over who had the best hair!

I love being a member of the club and I've made some lovely friends, especially Lucy, Birgitta and Arja. My dream is to watch the show being filmed one day. I think that would be fantastic".

Lisa and Sally celebrated their engagement on 25th May 2016. A fitting and fairy-tale ending for two of the most dedicated followers of Emmerdale – and what a lovely storyline. They are to be married in 2017.

Kirstyn Hume also attended the weekend in 2010: "I come from Jedburgh in the Scottish Borders and my mum Lorraine and I are avid fans of the show. We have attended several weekends and especially remember the bush planting ceremony to celebrate the club's 20th anniversary. I was

Kirstyn helps plant Magnolia Bush

honoured to give Jenny a helping hand to plant the magnolia bush in the garden of Mill Cottage.

Our favourite character in the programme was Stephanie Stokes (Lorraine Chase) and we loved chatting to her. She was always welcoming and great fun to talk to and a truly genuine and lovely person. We would love to see her return to the show one day.

It was always great to meet other fans of the show and the cast and crew are brilliant to everyone. We have great memories.

Well done Jenny and fellow members of this wonderful club".

Val Jones: "My first visit to Emmerdale was in 2009 and one of the first people I met was Angie Stanger-Leathes. I was made so welcome and when you are alone on your first weekend it is lovely to be looked after, and I was. I met another Angie too – Angie Reece, who was great fun (sadly no longer with us) but she had some lovely times at the weekends and I have warm memories of her. I also made friends with two other members, which was a great bonus for me.

Val in Emmerdale Post Office

I was thrilled to meet my favourite actors, Mark Charnock (Marlon), Jeff Hordley (Cain) and Steve Halliwell (Zak) – you can tell I like the Dingle family!

I attended as many weekends as possible after that and highlights for me are the gala dinner, and being able to visit the studios and the village. That first trip though will always be extra special for me. I remember standing behind the counter at the post office which at that time was run by Viv Windsor

(Deena). I also visited the factory which made curtains and in those days the sets were actually in the village itself and although they are no longer there, I think of them fondly.

I started watching the show in 1972 and still remember the very first episode. I still can't wait for it to start each weeknight evening. It is always so consistently brilliant and deserves the highest awards. I always thought that Eden Taylor-Draper (Belle) was a star in the making, and now we have Amelia Flanagan (April), who is a brilliant little actress too.

Congratulations to Jenny on reaching 25 years of the fan club and thanks to all the cast and crew who make the weekends so enjoyable".

Hannele Pakkala travelled from Finland to attend the club weekend in 2014:

"Emmerdale fan club weekend is about to start and I'm sitting on my bed in the Weetwood Hotel in Leeds. I'm thinking more and more about the magical atmosphere of these special times and this year the theme is 'The Great Gatsby' with 1920's style dresses. This is the third event for me and I am wondering if I will meet new cast

Hannele with Zoe Henry and Jeff Hordley

members or something new or different in the village this year. Now it is time to start the night of my dreams.

It is amazing to me that some of the actors and actresses can remember you from previous years. Their charm and charisma are very powerful and being in the same room as them is simply wonderful.

I think the world of Jeff Hordley (Cain) as he is so down to earth and he is very popular among the Finnish fans – especially the ladies! His real life wife Zoe, who plays Rhona in the show, always gives plenty of space for everyone to take photos of her real-life husband Jeff. She is one of my favourite characters. Joe Gill (Finn) is also worth a special mention.

The Emmerdale crew are always with us and I love that because they are so friendly and helpful. What does Emmerdale mean to me? It is an escape from normal and for a brief time each day I can be someone else and imagine I live in the village. It also teaches me English culture and language and the most important thing is meeting other fans who love the show as much as I do.

Congratulations to the fan club that is 25 years old now. May it have many more years in the future. I love you Emmerdale!"

Chapter 10

Bournemouth to Aberdeen via Belfast

C lub members Lucy Row and Birgitta Skattberg have attended cricket matches, theatre trips and charity events, supporting the cast whenever possible over the years. This is Lucy's story:

"This sounds like some road trip; it was, and still is….

I can't start to add up all the miles some of us have covered over the past 15 years. We've seen the cast play cricket, appear in theatre and do lots of adrenalin-rushing stunts - and simply daft things for charitable causes.

I need to go back and recall how we met and became friends. I also have to say it was our mutual admiration for the Vicar of Emmerdale that had a lot to do with it, as Ashley and Bernice became an item on screen. The internet was starting to grow, so Emmerdale/Soap related websites were appearing for likeminded fans to meet up online. It probably helped that most of us lived in the UK apart from Birgitta, who had been following Emmerdale for years back home in Sweden.

At the beginning, our mutual friend Gilly was studying at York University. She was the first of us to go to a charity cricket match at Harrogate featuring the Emmerdale team led by the one and only Chris Chittell (Eric Pollard). I still have her written account of that day and the opportunity there was to meet the Emmerdale team. I suppose that was the catalyst for the rest of us to meet up and go to cricket matches too, as and when we could. It was also an opportunity to meet up with other Emmerdale fan club members and on occasions, with support from Tim Fee and Jenny Godfrey, the fan club had a designated meeting point.

I talked to John Middleton (Rev Ashley Thomas) recently about the fan club book and about the cricket team he was involved with in the early years. There was one particular match we especially enjoyed watching at Ackworth. Emmerdale had won it in the last over and we were very vocal afterwards. He told me: "At school I was good at two sports, running and cricket, well… passable". As for his 'Catch of the Match' he said "I thought I came charging down to the crease, whipped in a fast straight ball and then made the most athletic and beautifully timed catch". Sadly he didn't! He saw our video clip of that last over and his run up was more like 'here comes the ambling vicar' and the catch looks like he's fallen over and got hit by the ball. Oh well, perceptions!

Going to matches was Birgitta's first experience of the UK and this game called cricket. I must mention Kez at this point, who was with us for many a journey, she was happy to drive absolutely anywhere. For the past 10 years Birgitta and I have continued our Emmerdale adventures by bus, train and even a plane to Belfast. One train journey to Chester was especially eventful; setting off from my house at 8 a.m. we missed our connection at Manchester due to engineering delays, meaning we didn't turn up for the cricket until 2 p.m. Thankfully Alli took pity on us, and with Chris Chittell's agreement, offered us a lift back to Leeds on the team bus. Needless to say we were more than happy and very grateful.

As the main man of the Emmerdale team, Chris Chittell has always been appreciative of the support we and many other fans have given the team over the years. Other cricket team regulars over the years include Frazer Hines, Patrick Mower and Matthew Wolfenden and I must mention just a couple of the crew, Roly Plant the cricket team's wicket-keeper and one time captain until he retired. He always came to see how we were doing. Also Prue Haynes aka 'The Commander', who kept the Emmerdale cast in order and has been known to play for the team as and when required.

Another team Emmerdale event and always a great weekend for us (apart from our fan club weekends) have been our trips to Aberdeen and Belfast. The cast are really good sports when it comes to joining in and taking part in charity events.

We had never thought of John Middleton as an adrenaline junkie! Yes he is, and the thing is we know he hates heights, so why did he do it? We have seen him zipping down a zip wire more than once. He told me: "The worst bit was hanging in the basket waiting to do it". He shared these thoughts on his high flying antics: "As for wing-walking, that's just so bizarre, it doesn't feel real. Strapped in and standing on the wing of the plane as it takes off, a voice in your head starts screaming at you. You've never been in a light aircraft before and you are stood on the wing. It's got a perfectly good seat, so what the chuffing hell are you doing?"

The worst thing John has ever done? Apparently it's abseiling down a 150ft tower: "It's like climbing over a five bar gate 150 feet up in the air and then dropping down, but in a controlled manner. I remember the bloke strapping me into a harness at the top and asking me how I got here today. Summoning up my self-control I managed to say "bus" and then he said 'Well that's probably the most dangerous thing you've done today'. "I couldn't respond - speech was beyond me".

I'll close by saying we are all part of something unique, no other soap has a fan club.

John remarked: "It's a chance for the cast to say thanks".

On Tour ......

Chapter 11

Fan Club 21ˢᵗ Birthday Celebrations

In January 2011 the members celebrated the club's 21st anniversary, which is testament to the dedication of Jenny Godfrey, and the continuing support of ITV, the management, cast and crew. As usual, Matt Cleary and his staff provided wonderful decorations for the special weekend and some very special memories for the fans:

Chris Pickering: "I have been in the Emmerdale fan club for around 10 years now and it has been a great part of my life. When I arrived for the first club weekend, Tim Fee was in charge and I thought he was a great organiser and he used to make sure everything in the village was open for us and I liked him very much.

Chris with friends Helen and Lee

The first person I had my photo taken with was Stan Richards (Seth Armstrong) and he was an amazing person to talk to – other fans used to get a bit fed up waiting for me to finish chatting to him but they were happy times. Many actors and actresses have come and gone over the years and one of my favourites was Patsy Kensit (Sadie King) and when I met her she was absolutely lovely and had time for everyone. The friends I have made on various weekends including Helen and Lee from Leicester are now friends for life and the folk from Finland are great fun too. I really love meeting up with them every year and also at other times. Angie and the rest of the fans I have met over the years have been wonderful and we have such fun at the club weekends and I can hardly wait for the next one.

The best experience for me with Emmerdale has to be when I became an 'extra' for the day. I had a full day in the village and the pub, working with such well known stars as Richard Thorp (Alan Turner) and Shirley Stelfox (Edna Birch), both of whom are sadly no longer with us. It was an unforgettable day for me and a wonderful experience. Also seeing some of the young actors and

actresses growing up such as Eden Taylor-Draper (Belle Dingle), make the show seem so believable. Eden has also been known to sing for us at club weekends, which was lovely to see and hear.

Chris with Ian Rowley and special effects

Throughout the 10 years I have seen many changes; not just to cast and crew but with the studio and village sets and it is really fascinating to see the different sets each time we visit.

Watching Ian Rowley and his amazing special effects has been another great treat for the fans – we even met Dusty Bin at his studio! The explosions and car crashes he demonstrated were nothing short of breathtaking – so clever how he makes things happen to such great effect.

Some of the actors stay in the bar with us after the gala dinner and socialising with the likes of Emily Symons, Danny Miller and Chris Chittell has been yet another highlight for me. To sum up – being a member of the Emmerdale fan club has been a fantastic experience for me and for so many other fans too. Thanks to Jenny who started the club – all of your efforts have certainly been worthwhile – so thanks for everything Jenny! The fan club is wonderful".

David Grimstone and **Emma Ticehurst** have attended many weekends together and David was also present at the 21st birthday celebrations. They shared these memories: "Firstly we want to offer our heartfelt congratulations to all involved with the Emmerdale Club for reaching the quarter century! Well done, it's a testament to your hard work and dedication.

We really enjoy coming to the weekends, seeing what happens behind the scenes in the studios and wandering around the village is a real treat. Meeting and chatting with cast and crew is fantastic.

David and Emma at Home Farm

For us the most treasured thing is the friendships we have forged with other members – really lovely, down to earth people. We would like to give a special mention here to Sue Mummery and her sons Michael and Thomas, who have become good friends and we often meet up with them at other times.

Long may this great club continue – see you all soon".

Suzanne McDonough joined the club in 2004 and has attended many weekends including the 21st anniversary celebrations. Suzanne loves to write poetry and has provided her memories in true poetic style!

Suzanne and 21st decorations

Magical Moments by Suzanne McDonough

Emmerdale here we come,
Memories to be made,
Making the most of our time,
Everything has been done,
Ready for the big weekend,
Dashes made from buses and trains,
As we all meet up again.
Lost in conversation and the thrill of it all,
Emmerdale fans just have a ball.

Sue Mummery and her sons **Michael and Thomas** have attended various weekends together and they told us: "We joined the club about 6 years ago and it was one of the best things we have ever done.

We have made lots of friends from all around the country and have met many of the cast members too. One who is special to us is Kitty McGeever (Lizzie) who is sadly no longer with us but she was lovely and we loved chatting to her.

Jenny organises the club very well and we all feel part of a special family. We feel very lucky to be part of such a special club and we love meeting old and new friends at the weekends. We also go and see some of the actors and actresses when they appear in theatre, and they include Charlie Hardwick (Val), Roxanne Pallett (Jo) and Claire King

Sue, Michael and Thomas Mummery with friends

(Kim). Thanks to all the cast, crew and fans who help make the weekends so very special".

Brian Moss and Maxine Williams also enjoyed the 21st celebrations: "Our Emmerdale experience started with Brian entering a competition in 2004 and we were delighted when he won second prize - the chance to attend a village barbeque party with the Emmerdale cast which also included overnight accommodation in a hotel in Leeds. The marquee was huge and there was a funfair, food and a free bar! We were also allowed to wander

into the village which needless to say we took advantage of! Our lasting memories of the event were chatting to Andy Devine (Shadrack) and thinking how well spoken he was, and seeing Jeff Hordley (Cain) having fun on the dodgems. We had a wonderful time and two very bad hangovers!

Brian and Maxine at Gala Dinner

A few years later we joined the fan club and were delighted to discover a club weekend in Leeds where we could visit the sets and the village and meet the cast too. We attended the 2009 weekend and have attended every one since then. Over the years as well as meeting many of the cast and crew, we have made friends with some of our fellow fans and we love staying at the Weetwood Hotel. Every weekend is unique and different with new cast to meet, new sets to see and new members to talk to. We loved seeing Ian Rowley too, and the special effects he demonstrated to us in the village. We have experienced all kinds of weather, sun, rain and snow – we have seen it all. We have just returned from the 25th anniversary weekend and it was as enjoyable and magical as our first one.

We are very proud to be part of the Emmerdale family – because that's what it is and we hope the show will continue to go from strength to strength, win many more deserved awards and we hope our fan club will prosper and go on forever".

Ann-Marie von Wowern travelled from her home in Sweden to her first club weekend in 2011 to celebrate 21 years of the show: "Since Emmerdale was first shown in Sweden in 1976 I have loved the show. I loved the Yorkshire landscape and had dreams of travelling to the dales and even meeting some of the actors. For me it was an almost impossible dream but I searched the internet and to my delight I discovered there was a UK fan club that I could join. After

Ann-Marie with Mark Charnock in Woolpack

joining I was lucky enough to be accepted for the club weekend in 2011 which was also the 21st anniversary of the show. 2011 became my lucky year. I flew to Leeds from Amsterdam and when I stepped into the Weetwood Hotel I felt my dream had come true. The decorations were wonderful with lots of 21st anniversary balloons and tinsel which made a great party atmosphere.

I met my idol Mark Charnock (Marlon) in the Woolpack which I could hardly believe. It was a magical experience and when I visited the village I could not believe I was in the same place as the actors in my favourite show.

In 2012 I was lucky enough again to be able to experience the magic. It was great to see familiar faces including Helen Spencer and Lee Boyall-Love who are lovely people. I am also friends on facebook with many members including some from Finland. We share many emotions over the internet so thanks to all of you.

I send my very best wishes to Jenny for her tremendous commitment and planning of these special weekends. Thank you Jenny for a fantastic club.

Finally a big thank-you to Angie Stanger-Leathes for letting me share my big dream by being part of the fan club book".

21st Anniversary Fan Club Badge

Chapter 12

40 Years of Emmerdale – and a 'Live' Show

On 17th October 2012 history was made in celebration of 40 years of the show being broadcast. A 'live' episode – an hour long on screen – was televised to millions of viewers as the cast and crew made history in Emmerdale village.

The Director for the history making episode was Tony Prescott, who had worked on 'live' episodes of Coronation Street, but this was a very different challenge as most of the scenes were to be set outside with the cast and crew exposed to the elements on a cold, October evening. The village was packed with 61

Matt Cleary ready to go 'live' in the Control Room

cast members and more than 70 crew in attendance. The fast moving, hour long episode featured two births, two weddings and a murder. There were gasps of surprise when the victim turned out to be Carl King (Tom Lister) – very few saw that coming! Even the wedding of Katie and Declan had a smattering of violence when Megan pushed Katie's face into the wedding cake! This was a high octane episode, the likes of which the fans had never seen before. A fitting tribute to celebrate 40 wonderful years.

Matt Cleary, Head of Production at Emmerdale, was at the centre of the action and was happy to share his special memories: "Wednesday, 17th October 2012 is a date that will stick in my mind for the rest of my life. This was the day that Emmerdale went 'live' for the very first time.

When I arrived at Emmerdale in 2009, everybody said that it couldn't be done. We'd seen other 'soaps' do live shows to celebrate their various anniversaries, but because the Emmerdale village and the studios are 8 miles apart, the practicalities of going 'live' were considered too great to overcome. To me this sounded like a challenge that the Emmerdale team were more than capable of delivering, so we put our heads together, came up with a plan and tentatively suggested to ITV that our 40th anniversary was the ideal opportunity to put this into action.

What I remember most from doing the 'live' episode is how the Emmerdale team worked together to get through a really demanding and pressurised production experience. At the end of the day, when you've got 10 million people watching you do your job, nobody wants to fluff a line, miss a shot, or do anything that is seen to let the rest of the team down.

Our brilliant Director, Tony Prescott, explained to our cast and crew that he'd divided the village up into different stages. For example, there was the hospital set built in the Village Hall, the B&B, the marquee and so on. Everyone who was working on the production only needed to think about their individual elements and not worry about what was happening in other parts of the village. It was Tony's job to tie everything together along with his gallery crew who would cut between scenes and make sure everything ran to time. This meant that the actors and crew only had to practice their own 3 minute scenes and be ready for action when the 1st Assistant Director gave them the signal.

Many of our actors and crew have worked on 'live' productions in the past and it was brilliant to watch them mentor their younger colleagues who had never done this sort of work before. Everyone pulled together and made things happen – it really was a team effort.

My own memories of the night are many, but the thing I remember most is the overwhelming feeling of adrenalin in the run-up to going on air. I can still remember the Script Supervisor saying the words, 'On air in 60 seconds and then counting down from 10,9,8 … the titles rolling and then that was it, my job was over. There was nothing I could do from this point on as it was now down to the cast and crew to put into practice everything they had been doing over and over again in the 2 weeks of rehearsals beforehand. All I could do was sit, watch, and hope everything went to plan.

You could have heard a pin drop from where I was watching in the Control Room with the show's then Producer, Stuart Blackburn and Executive Producers, Steve November and John Whiston. We hung on every cue, every shot and every word. I felt like time had stood still apart from what was happening on the bank of screens in front of us.

As we got to the first commercial break with a flawless performance, the pressure seemed to lift just a little. The second commercial break came and went as did the third. So far everything was perfect and we only had a few minutes left before I could finally breathe again. With relief the last line on the script was spoken and a voice came through to tell us that we were now 'off air'. Phew!

The celebrations went on long into the night. The cast and crew had delivered an impeccable 'live' episode, worthy of the 40 years of brilliant work that their predecessors had done making the 6,370 episodes that preceded it. I'm so proud to have been a part of it, and so proud of the team for doing such an amazing job. It was a pleasure to raise a glass to Emmerdale along with Jenny Godfrey and Angie Stanger-Leathes who had come along to represent the fans, before heading home with a huge sense of achievement for a well

Jenny in marquee with wedding flowers after the 'live'

deserved rest".

Some of the cast and crew who worked on the 'live' show shared their experiences:

Nick Miles: "The thing about the 'live' episode was the constant sense of teetering on the edge of disaster. Nobody had ever attempted a 'live' as an outside broadcast and some of the locations were as much as a quarter of a mile from other parts of the village. Not one of the rehearsals went completely according to plan and even as we did the broadcast I remember a camera having no electricity less than 30 seconds before it went 'live'! The overall experience was thrilling but in quite a scary way. It was a brilliant night".

Bhasker Patel: "A magical and a once in a lifetime experience as nothing went wrong".

Tom Lister: "It was the most incredible episode, I couldn't have asked after 9 years of being on the show to go out in that fashion. It was just amazing and we were all thrilled with how it went".

Peter Hancock: "I worked on the Emmerdale 'live' episode as a 3rd Assistant

Angie with Jeff Hordley after the show

Director. The 3rd choreographs all the supporting artistes and helps the 1st A.D. control the floor. On the 'live' I was in the B & B where 'Gennie' gave birth and on the night we had 2 newborns on standby outside in a caravan behind the Woolpack. One of my jobs was to rush out in the two scenes gap before we cut back to the B & B and choose which of the babies should be taken onto the set – basically, which one I thought would be quietest. As soon as 'Carl King' had been hit around the head with the infamous brick, off we went on set to wait for the next B & B scene. As the closing scene began and the titles started to roll, the baby started to bawl its head off. I think I just about got away with it!"

Tony Audenshaw and 'White Van Man' Band entertain the fans

Dean Wright: "I love being involved with the fan club because everyone is so friendly and always keen to learn and listen to everything we share with them.

The 'live' episode was as thrilling as a roller-coaster ride for me. I was supervising in the hospital set where 'Debbie Dingle' was giving birth. We had a huge flow of emotion when we finally conquered the challenge".

Fan club member **Angie Stanger-Leathes** was lucky enough to witness the 'live' show: "Thank you Jenny Godfrey and ITV! It was such an important occasion and a huge achievement for the cast and crew producing wonderfully professional performances from everyone. As we were being transported to the village to witness the 'live' proceedings, I couldn't help thinking how totally nerve-wracking it must be for each and every one of them, knowing that millions of viewers were watching for every tiny flaw and with normal working rules flying out of the window!

We were shown into 'Eric and Val's' barn home where management and guests of ITV had gathered. A few lucky fan club members had won a competition to attend the broadcast and there was a real sense of history being made that evening. We watched the show on large screens in the building and it was unreal to think the drama that was unfolding was happening just a short distance from where we were situated. The storylines were absolutely breathtaking with high drama at every turn – two births, two weddings and a death – all in one episode. It was mind-boggling!

Celebrating 40 years of Emmerdale

After the cameras stopped rolling, Alli took us to the giant marquee that was used for the wedding of 'Declan and Katie'. We sipped champagne and everyone could relax at last. The cast and crew did a brilliant job and there was huge relief all round afterwards. The village had a magical and mysterious feel to it in the darkness after the show and I managed to walk down Main Street for a few moments and experience the magic. What a privilege it was and an experience I will never forget. Thank you Emmerdale and thank you ITV".

The following month, November, was the fan club weekend and the celebration of 22 years of the club. On the Saturday morning trip to the studios some of the sets were dressed in Christmas decorations as Christmas and New Year episodes had just been filmed. That evening at the gala dinner, Chris Chittell (Eric) and Matthew Wolfenden (David) auctioned some items including a day at the studios watching filming, all in aid of the 'Text Santa' charity appeal. Raising funds for charity has always been part of the weekend activities and club members can be rightly proud of the monies they have raised over the years for various charitable causes. We were then entertained by the fantastic Tony Audenshaw (Bob) and his colourful band 'White Van Man'. Tony is an accomplished singer and the fans danced the night away along with some of the cast and crew. Another wonderful gala dinner and dance night for the fans to savour.

On Sunday, after a wonderful trip to the village, the fans returned to the hotel for their farewell Sunday lunch and were delighted to be joined by cast members including Gaynor Faye (Megan), Laura Norton (Kerry), Bhasker Patel (Rishi) and Will Johnson (Dominic). Then it was time to say goodbye and pay homage to another fantastic club weekend. 2012 had been a momentous year for the show and it was wonderful for the fan club members to feel such a special part of it.

Chapter 13

Over the Sea and Far Away Places

M any club members face long journeys from all parts of the UK and overseas to meet up in Leeds for the special weekends. Across the Irish sea to the city of Cork is our first stop for more special memories:

Ralph with Louise Appleton

Ralph O'Flaherty: "The very first of these wonderful fan weekends my mum Chrissie and I attended was in 2008 and we felt it was just too good to be true! As Friday, 8th February rolled around, the excitement and the nerves mounted, as we eagerly travelled to the Weetwood Hotel. We had flown from Cork to Leeds and what a warm welcome awaited us. At this point I must mention that the staff and crew of the show were all wonderful to us – so helpful, kind and friendly and all done in their own time. So a huge thank you to those guys.

After arriving in the bar and having a few sips of wine, things started to get really exciting when Tim Fee announced that several of the cast members would call in to see us that Friday evening after filming. Chatting with Steve Halliwell, Dominic Brunt and Chris Villiers was fantastic. The hilarious Chris Chittell also arrived and informed us he was off on a charity walk to the Andes the following morning. These folk were so generous with their time and we were truly appreciative of that.

Chrissie with Chris Chittell

Afterwards at dinner, we made some new friends, Heather and Dennis who lived near London and were also on their first trip to Emmerdale.

The following morning was full of delights with a trip to the studios which was so interesting. When we arrived in the 'Woolpack', who pops out from behind the bar but Tony Audenshaw! He had made a special effort to be there as he could not make the gala dinner that evening. He posed for photos and chatted and full credit to him – it was a huge treat for the fans.

We also met the lovely Val Lawson who showed us the prison, the police station and the hospital – she was so full of enthusiasm and we were delighted with all the facts she told us about the show.

The gala dinner was fantastic, wonderful food followed by a charity auction hosted by Patrick Mower and ably assisted by his onscreen son and daughter, Nicola Wheeler and Matthew Bose. These three transformed an ordinary auction into such a floorshow – it was so entertaining!

The following day, Sunday, we were to meet the biggest star of the show, well in physical size anyhow – the village! A quick stroll down the hill and there we were on Main Street, Emmerdale – oh my God! We were allowed to wander into the B & B, the church, the vets and the village hall. It is impossible to describe the excitement of being there and even the graveyard had me feeling emotional which is testament to the power of this wonderful show. After lunch at the hotel, we said our goodbyes to our new found friends, Heather and Dennis, Linda and Vanessa, Kath and Elaine, Angie, John, Shirley from Dublin and too many more to mention!

Now in 2016, the weekends are as exciting as the first one. They are now as much about seeing old friends again as they are about seeing all things Emmerdale.

We have been extremely lucky to have won the chance to visit the studios during working days, so we were privileged to see the cast and crew doing what they do best, filming our beloved show.

We are both so grateful to Jenny Godfrey for running the club and making all this possible and we want to thank the terrific cast and crew for all they do for us. Thank you, thank you, thank you!"

Shirley Kerrigan hails from Dublin and is always the 'life and soul of the party' at club weekends, despite having mobility problems and needing to travel from Dublin Airport to Leeds/Bradford and back again. 'Shirl the girl' is always smiling and is a colourful personality, much loved by cast and crew and

Shirley with trademark glass of wine!

her fellow members. Never short of a word for anyone and full of witty one-liners: "Where to start with my memories of the fan club is a hard one. The first year I went to a weekend I was on crutches and just wanted to have something different and exciting to do. I arrived at the Weetwood Hotel with my suitcase and glad rags!

Everyone was so warm and welcoming to me and before long I knew plenty of the club members. The first cast member I met was 'bad boy' Cain Dingle (the lovely Jeff Hordley). I can still remember it all with great fondness. My first club weekend was 11 years ago and I celebrated my 50th birthday with my Emmerdale friends in 2014. I love meeting old friends and making new ones too each year.

My first memories of watching the show were in 1972 when we first acquired a TV set. I remember sitting on a couch in our back room to watch with my mum and dad and sister. I loved the show from the very beginning and have done so ever since. From then on it was my dream to visit the village and meet the cast. Never in my wildest dreams did I think it would ever happen but when I joined the fan club, my dreams turned into reality. I never expected to be able to attend so many weekends and I also had a great trip to Aberdeen one year when the cast were there for a charity event and we all stayed in the same hotel. A few other club members were there too and a great time was had by all.

I have made lovely friends and I want to thank everyone; fans, cast and crew and especially Jenny for giving me memories that money just can't buy".

Michael Barnes is another fan from across the Irish sea: "I joined the club in 2012 as I don't live in England and felt it was my best chance to sample the full Emmerdale experience. On my first weekend I was made to feel welcome by Jenny and Angie and met plenty of other friendly members.

My favourite cast members are Chris Chittell, Matthew Wolfenden and Adam Fielding, who has now left the show.

I always look forward to the special weekends which are now as much about seeing good friends as about meeting the cast and visiting the indoor and outdoor sets. I love to see the changes in the sets, with Home Farm seeing the most changes. I also like hearing about new arrivals in the show, such as Vanessa and the White family and finding out more about how episodes are filmed such as when Chas and Debbie were trapped in the cellar with Cameron.

Michael on the famous bridge

The weekends are similar in format but every effort is made to ensure there are different experiences to enjoy each time so every year is different to the previous one. I feel lucky to have attended 4 weekends already as they are very popular and a must for any fan of the show.

I like Emmerdale because it has some of the nicest cast members who do good work for charity, and it is the best 'soap' for humour and at dealing with such emotional stories such as baby Daniel's death and Aaron being abused.

Thanks to Jenny and all the cast and crew for making it so very special for the fans".

Sandra Kaun travelled overseas from her home in Sweden and said: "Emmerdale has always been in my life. My mother Eva has followed the show from the start. I didn't always watch it as a child but it was there in the background. I have watched it regularly since the age of 17.

A few years ago we decided it would be lovely to visit the real village so I checked online and discovered the fan club. We joined and were very pleased to perhaps be able to make our dream come true. Jenny was very helpful and we attended our first club weekend in 2013. It was wonderful and we could hardly believe how many cast and crew gave up their time for us.

To see how the show is made and see the lighting and cameras is so impressive and interesting. When we returned home to Sweden my brother Mats and my aunt Mija joined the club and in 2014 we were all given places on the weekend. My brother loved meeting his favourite cast member Jeff Hordley as he loves the character, Cain Dingle. We actually think they look quite similar. We loved the trip and last year I bought an Emmerdale

Sandra in Emmerdale village

tee shirt but it was stolen from my car. My mother created a replacement for me and one for my brother so the story ended happily.

We are fans of the best show in the world which takes such good care of us too. It is great to meet the different fans from around the world and thanks to everyone for making our weekends so wonderful".

Two fans from Canada and New Zealand have not been able to attend club weekends due to living so far away, but they want to share their thoughts of what it means to be club members:

Lourice Hines: "I started watching the show in 2001 on a Canadian broadcasting channel. After watching a few episodes I was hooked. What struck me then about the show and still does today, is its special uniqueness. I like how it takes in not just characters doing dialogue but includes the village and its country surroundings which adds so much to the overall feel of the programme. I find it riveting to watch and the storylines are very interesting.

I joined the fan club in 2011 and I really enjoy being a member because of the privileges it brings. I have a

Lourice and her special tea towel

binder which has become packed with material from the club and I love receiving the newsletters. I was thrilled to win a 40th anniversary tea towel which I won in a club competition and it is very special to me.

I also gained a friend right after becoming a member. The newsletter has a pen-pal section and I met Karen Place from Middlesbrough and we email regularly and chat on the phone and discuss the storylines which is lovely.

I also enjoy being in touch with the organiser Jenny, and I am delighted to be a member of such a wonderful fan club family".

Jane Lavery: "I live in the Rakaia Gorge in the South Island of New Zealand and I have been watching Emmerdale for more years than I care to remember. My husband and I both love the show and watching the dramas unfold in the village. I joined the fan club a few years ago and love receiving the newsletters and in one of the competitions I won an Emmerdale tea towel which was produced to celebrate 40 years of the show. Not long afterwards my husband and I were going on a trip overseas and I thought it best to put my affairs in order by making a Will. When I told our daughter she told me she definitely wanted the tea towel so it has now become an heirloom which will hopefully give people a bit of a laugh when the time comes for the reading of the Will.

One of the things I would love to do on my travels is take part in an Emmerdale weekend and it is on my wish list of places to visit. I would love to be an 'extra' in the Woolpack, having a drink in the background or walking through the door to the toilets, where everyone seems to share their deepest secrets and thinks no one is listening!

I look forward to watching Emmerdale and being part of the fan club for many years to come".

Jane with her Emmerdale heirloom!

Chapter 14

Special Friends and Precious Moments

Many club members have formed close friendships with other fans and experienced some poignant moments over the years:

Steve Marshall: "The Emmerdale Fan Club is truly unique, the fact it has celebrated 25 years and is still going strong is a great credit to Jenny Godfrey and Tim Fee who created such a special club and today their legacy keeps it special for the fans. The continued support from Matt, Alli, the Emmerdale team and ITV, ensures Emmerdale offers a club no other 'soap' provides and I've enjoyed all the opportunities to support the club through the years.

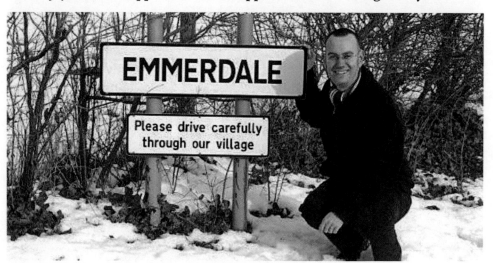

Steve in a snowy Emmerdale village

I remember my first weekend arriving at the Weetwood finding the room was not ready and sitting down in the reception area not knowing anybody but sensing that the groups of people who had gathered had come to meet the cast of Emmerdale and visit the studios and village. I still remember sitting on one of the sofas, picking up a newspaper, pretending to read it and quietly observing what was going on. One lady kept making eye contact with me. I disappeared back into the newspaper (probably reading it upside down or not even knowing what I was reading) and then the lady asked if I was there for the Emmerdale weekend and was I on my own and would I like to join them? That lady was the lovely June Brown and from that moment I was welcomed into the friendship circle of June Brown, Bryan Dickson, Jenny Dutton, Geoff Dixon and Norman & Irene Cooper and we spent the next few hours discussing what was about to happen on the weekend, their experiences of visiting that village that the general public could not access and discussing Emmerdale in general. At the gala dinner I had the pleasure to sit next to Susan Hartley and we instantly clicked and chatted all evening and from that weekend the years have passed, and some great friendships have been formed. We have had so many laughs along the way, it is true after every weekend, a day is required to recover from all the laughter and banter we have.

Many years ago Susan had the idea following the Friday evening dinner and episode to do a pub quiz to try and get new members involved with the more established members and it has been a pleasure to construct the picture quiz and really put the experts to the test with 43 years of knowledge needed. The archivist also provides some tricky questions putting us fans under pressure! Thanks to everyone who has taken part over the years and kept Susan and myself busy with the marking and it's great to see such a competitive group of fans competing to be champions.

Two things will always stand out for me as a member of the club. The initial one is the first time I entered the Emmerdale village, I still recall the drive down the access road on the bus, wondering where on earth we were heading. Then that wow moment when you walk down the hill, turn the corner and see the picturesque village is a dream come true and so mind- blowing to realise you are actually standing in Main Street - the very place so many of our favourite artistes have acted out their scenes.

The second stand out moment was attending Richard Thorp's Memorial Service at Leeds Cathedral in October 2013 and I was honoured to perform a reading on behalf of Jenny and the club in front of Richard's family and the Emmerdale cast & crew.

Our club is exceptional, with the newsletters, special events, lunches and the highlight of the year, the weekends. To meet the cast, visit the studios, village and other locations is a great privilege and the crew are fantastic from Props, Script, AD's, Writers etc. who all give up their time to let us ask all the questions and delve behind the scenes of ITV".

Tosh and Debbie Tolond have been members for more than 5 years and Debbie has these memories: "My first experience of an Emmerdale weekend

Debbie and Tosh - Emmerdale style!

was in 2011 for the 21st anniversary of the fan club. I went with just my mum and dad, Ann and John as my husband Tosh couldn't make it that year. We went again in 2014 and this time Tosh was able to join us. We absolutely loved every minute and we also attended in 2016 for the 25th anniversary, Hollywood style! I have really enjoyed being a member of the fan club from attending the weekends and two London lunches, to meeting new people, making new friends and of course meeting the cast and crew of Emmerdale. Jenny is the lynch-pin of all this; running the fan club with efficiency and at the same time becoming a friend, someone you can chat to about the show or anything else that takes your fancy. I've only known Jenny for about 5 years but in that time she has made me feel very welcome at all of the events I've attended. I think she does an amazing job in making the fan club the fun place it is".

Janice and Steve Wilson attended their first weekend in 2014 although they have been fans of the show from the very early days. Janice said: "I have been a huge fan of Emmerdale since the very beginning. My husband Steve has only become hooked in the last few years, but is as mad about it as I am now! We didn't realise there was a fan club until a couple of years ago and we joined as soon as we found out about it. We were then lucky enough to attend our first Emmerdale weekend in 2014 (for my 60th birthday) and what

Janice and Steve at the Woolpack

a fabulous time we had! The whole weekend from Friday to Sunday was packed with so many different things. On the Friday evening we met some of the stars of the show. Without exception they were all so friendly and welcoming. By the end of the evening everyone was on first name terms and I felt we had become part of a special family. We were also able to watch that night's episode so that was wonderful too.

On Saturday we went to the studios and were shown around the sets and in the afternoon we went to see the Props department. Steve was in his element seeing all the props used in the show and then the best was to come at the gala dinner when many more cast joined us. We had a fantastic evening and lots of money was raised for charitable causes in the auction. A disco afterwards with a Beatles tribute group to entertain us – brilliant!

On Sunday we were taken to the village which is tucked away from prying eyes at the back of a farm. That was an experience in itself, walking down Main Street and having a photo taken outside the 'Woolpack'.

The whole experience was beyond our wildest expectations. We have made lots of wonderful friends and facebook connections made with many of them. We can't wait to see all our friends again".

Sonia and Paul Woodford attended their first club weekend in 2014 and successfully bid at the charity auction to win a VIP tour. Sonia recalls: "It all started with a fabulous Emmerdale weekend in October 2014. We loved it so much, there was no stopping Paul bidding for the Emmerdale VIP tour at the fundraising gala dinner.

It was us and another family in the bidding which became quite high, but eventually we won the prize. We had a chat with Alli afterwards and decided to split the winning bid between us and the other family so we could all go, which was lovely.

In January 2015 we stayed at the Weetwood Hotel

Sonia and Paul with Liz Estensen

the night before our tour and we travelled around 100 miles from our home in Buckinghamshire, full of anticipation and excitement. A taxi arrived to take us to the studios where we were met by Alli who showed us around and all the while we were eagerly looking to see who we could spot! In the canteen we met some of the cast including Chris Chittell (Eric) and Meg Johnson (Pearl) and then we were allowed to watch some rehearsals in the salon and afterwards Laura Norton (Kerry) came over to see us and Paul was chuffed that she remembered him from the weekend in October!

Back to the canteen for a delicious lunch (so much choice!) where we desperately, but unsuccessfully tried to find out more about upcoming storylines from the crew members. We also met the Head of Production, Matt Cleary, who also remembered us from October. A few cast members including Matthew Wolfenden (David) and Natalie Anderson (Alicia) posed for photos with us and everyone was very friendly.

After a tour of the Props store it was off in Alli's car to the village. Alli is amazing, explaining everything, answering all of our questions (avoiding storylines!) and answering her constantly ringing phone! It was absolutely freezing in the village and flakes of snow were falling so Alli lent me her spare coat and I felt quite important wandering around the village in an official ITV fleece. We went into the Grange B & B and watched a film crew as they prepared for yet another scene. Then it was off to the village hall for a much needed hot chocolate and a reluctant goodbye to Alli as our taxi arrived to take us back to the hotel. We had an amazing time and special thanks to Alli and everyone we met that day.

None of this would have been possible if it wasn't for Jenny running the fan club and organising so much for the members – a big thank you to Jenny too!

PS – the next day Samantha Giles (Bernice) put a photo of the village on twitter absolutely covered in snow, so I think we went just in time!"

Pete and Samantha Bone also joined in 2014 and attended their first weekend in 2016. They recall: "This was our first year attending the weekend and we were completely blown away by the effort, organisation, friendliness and time that was put into making this weekend so very special – it was brilliant!

Both the cast and the crew went above and beyond and the access given to us on the sets and at the village was fantastic. At no point were we ever made to feel as though anything was too much trouble. Everyone did their utmost to ensure a seamless, fun and informative weekend for all of us. We have never attended anything like this before, and given the chance we would definitely love to come back again. The hotel and the food were wonderful and the efforts of the staff shone through.

Finally, we would both like to say a huge thank you to Jenny, as without her dedication and diligence, none of this would be possible. Thank you for organising such a wonderful, jam-packed, fun-filled weekend, and we want to thank the cast and crew for making it so special. Thank you all – it was perfect!"

Pete and Samantha relax on set

Chapter 15

Magical Tunes, Kiwi Madness and 'Mum's The Word'

As the opening credits roll for each new episode and the viewers eagerly await the latest dramas in the dales, the introductory theme tune is as familiar as the show itself, and has been since the show was first aired in 1972.

The creator of that famous theme is one of the most gifted composers and songwriters of his generation, and he has also written themes for other shows.

Tony Hatch is that famous composer, and he said: "I'm extremely proud to have been associated with Emmerdale since the very beginning. That was 1972.

First, I was asked if I would like to submit an idea for a theme. How could I say 'no'? Then I was given a 'storyboard' of the opening titles, which is a bit like a cartoon with several boxes showing various scenes. For Emmerdale Farm (as it was then) the scenes were of rolling dales, stone

Tony Hatch, creator of the Emmerdale theme tune

walls, a village pub and a farmhouse. I also received hints on how the scenes might be edited plus some titles superimposed on the scenes. This gave me an idea for the pace of the opening sequence. I looked at the illustrations and immediately went to my piano and started playing. What followed began in a minor key and gradually ended up with positive major chords. I only ever wrote the one theme.

Yorkshire Television loved the idea and we recorded the music in London late in 1971. The budget was small (5 musicians) but that worked in my favour because I could concentrate on the sole sounds of the oboe and the harp accompanied by a guitar, piano and bass. It has gone through quite a few changes since then but it is still Emmerdale and although I am no longer mentioned in the credits, it seems everyone knows it's my theme anyway.

I think the best version of the theme was recorded a few years ago when a wonderful promo video was produced for ITV that showed the cast coming to life through a Renaissance painting. It had a big orchestral sound and was brilliant!

I've been pretty lucky writing themes for long-running shows; 'Crossroads' (after 22 years) is no longer on our screens, but of course 'Neighbours' rolls on and I have a feeling 'Emmerdale' will be around for many more years to come.

Congratulations to Jenny and the fan club members for 25 years of total dedication".

Who would have thought that an ambassador for the Government of New Zealand would have even heard of Emmerdale? It's true though and Jenny was delighted to bestow honorary membership on one of New Zealand's most colourful characters, **Sir Peter Charles Leitch**, (also known as 'The Mad Butcher') who was delighted to share memories of his visits to the dales: "To say I am an Emmerdale fan is an understatement. I'm a tragic, never missing an episode.

I travelled to England with the New Zealand Rugby League team – 'The Kiwis'- in November 2015. I recorded every episode so when I arrived home after 6 weeks away I was able to have an Emmerdale marathon.

I've been to see the set, and when I am in Leeds I always visit the studios, and whenever I do, the cast members have always been superb – down to earth, charming and obliging.

Sir Peter with Kelvin Fletcher and 'Warriors' shirt

I'm lucky to have come to know Jenny, the club founder, and we even met up in London once and had afternoon tea. I've also become friends with Alli Piggott, who handles PR.

The first time I met anyone from the cast it also involved Rugby League. I was in Leeds with the Kiwis and we were having a drink. Two girls came over to meet the players because they were big fans. We got talking and Emmerdale came up in conversation and it turned out they had a friend in the show. They called her up and she joined us and we had a wonderful time. Since it involved a few drinks, I will keep her identity secret, but it was a real highlight for me.

On New Zealand TV they once did a *This Is Your Life* show about me and it included a pre-recorded slot from Emmerdale's James Hooton (Sam Dingle) thanking me for being such a big fan.

So why do I love Emmerdale? I love the storylines, which are always so real and often about our sense of community. My favourite character has to be

Andy Sugden (Kelvin Fletcher) mainly because Kelvin is such a huge fan of rugby league. On my last visit (with the Kiwis in 2015) I presented him with a 'Vodaphone Warriors' jersey, (they are my club in New Zealand).

Yes indeed, I have two big passions in life, Rugby League and Emmerdale, and even I am not certain which one comes first!

25 years of the fan club – I'll drink to that, cheers everyone".

Two more special people have had a big involvement with the fan club since it was founded in 1990. As a mum with 2 young sons, club founder Jenny attended most club events with her boys, Robert and Michael. Ever since they can remember, the fan club has been part of their lives and now as adults they want to share some memories of their Emmerdale experiences:

Robert Godfrey: "For virtually as long as I can remember my mum has run the Emmerdale fan club. The launch at London Zoo, going to see cast members in pantomimes and even making one of our childhood favourites 'Sooty' an honorary member, and of course the club weekends, have been a special part of my life.

Visiting the film studios with stairs in the houses going nowhere always intrigued me as a child, and if we were lucky we bumped into a cast member or two. When Emmerdale built the village I was surprised and impressed how quickly it was built and how it was constructed in an empty field – a real brick built village yet it was a film set for a TV show.

My mum has worked hard running the club over the past 25 years, organising the weekends, writing newsletters and dealing with the day to day running of the club including fan mail. The club is great for fans of the programme to actually interact with other fans, the cast and crew and visit the places they watch on television".

Michael Godfrey: "My mum, Jenny Godfrey, started the club pretty much as I was born. In what I consider quite an audacious move, with two young kids and a husband who spent much of his life working at sea, my mum saw an opportunity and took it upon herself to contact the production team of her favourite TV show to propose that she starts a club to serve the fans of Britain's best loved village. I was far too young to remember, but I suspect she was somewhat surprised to end up at London Zoo with Stan Richards and other cast members at the launch of 'The Official Emmerdale Fan Club'.

Some of my earliest memories are at Emmerdale. Those of you who have been on a club weekend will know it as a modern, slick, fast paced and well-oiled TV production machine, but in the early days it was a different dynamic with less episodes to produce and in far different locations. For instance I remember when it was filmed in an old mill. As a toddler too young to actually appreciate the special substance of the weekend, I remember being passed around different departments 'helping' (interfering!) with make-up, being sat in the Director's chair and being shown camera set-ups and how things work. Those amazing people at Emmerdale probably had no idea of the memories they were making not only for me, but for fans who had spent their time and money on visiting their place of work which, to those devoted fans, was the most magical place on earth.

Both my mum and the staff of Emmerdale gave up their own weekends to take us around the studios, visit locations (back then it was filmed in Esholt) and spend time socialising with fans to give them the opportunity to meet the real life people behind the fictional characters that enter their homes on most days, rain or shine. The show offers a form of escapism from daily life which for many can sometimes be extremely tough. For such a large organisation to open their doors to their true devoted fans is not only inspiring, but is a testament to how kind-hearted and good natured the Emmerdale team were, and still are to this day.

My visits to Emmerdale gave me and the other fans the opportunity to see the magic of TV production. At the time, the show was the only mainstream UK 'soap' to show such commitment to their fans which even led to them winning 'Britain's Fan Friendliest Soap'. Brookside and Eastenders didn't enjoy the same privilege as the awesome fans of Emmerdale who make the show what it is. For my mum, it's almost a full-time job – our house was often overrun with newsletters, envelopes, printers, seating plans, itineraries and stamps during the rush to get newsletters from print to paper, despatch to delivery and to organise the club weekends. I think many fans think there is a big team behind the club but the day to day running of it has always been just my mum on her own, but of course not without the considerable support of the ITV staff, cast and crew.

Both the staff and fans of Emmerdale have watched me and my brother grow up. Now at 28 years old, I've realised that I have also watched them grow and excel through their respective careers. My first memories of Tim Fee are those of a man at the 'helm of the ship', responsible for everything at Emmerdale and always busy. I've seen Roly Plant devote time to seeing these weekends through, rushing around with supplies and auction prizes. Val Lawson has always been amazing with the fans and watching Alli Piggott selling lots of memorabilia in the Emmerdale shop is another lasting memory.

So when I say I've grown up with Emmerdale, I really have. From being sat on Stan Richards' knee in the 'Woolpack', being patched up by then Producer Morag Bain when I'd fallen over and grazed my knee, looking at old scripts from the plane crash days and seeing devoted fans from all walks of life coming together to share the special weekend experience – it's all been an amazing experience.

So thank you to everyone who didn't just give up a few hours here and there for fans – this is much more than that. Thank you for all the work you do and have done to provide fans with the awesome experiences over 25 years.

And, lastly, thank you to my amazing mum, Jenny Godfrey. Thank you for being so devoted, for showing me the magic of TV and a true work ethic, for showing me that ideas can be turned into reality and that nothing is unachievable. My mum started this club and has run it whilst being a single mum for the last 20+ years and through her devotion, she's provided this opportunity for fans and for us as a family. The Emmerdale staff are amazing at what they do and have supported my mum entirely, but without her there would be no club, there would be no fan club weekend and my life, and the lives of many fans would have been totally different. Thank you to everyone at Emmerdale for providing me, my family and fans with some amazing memories and life experiences, and thank you to my mum for everything you do. You're the absolute bestest and I've had an amazing childhood watching you do something you love doing, and making the club what it is today. Thank you".

Top left and right: Robert and Michael wearing their fan club tee shirts and with Stan Richards in the Woolpack

Bottom left and right: The boys with honorary member 'Sooty' and Emmerdale fan club members

Chapter 16

25th Anniversary Celebrations – Hollywood Style!

The fan club celebrated its 25th birthday in January 2015 – an extraordinary and unique achievement, and Matt Cleary decided that Jenny's work and commitment over the years must be celebrated. And what a celebration that turned out to be!

On 2nd December 2015, Jenny was invited to the studios to celebrate the special anniversary and never in her wildest dreams did she imagine what a special day it would be. Along with a few fan club members Jenny was taken to the village where Chris Chittell and Gaynor Faye were waiting to greet her, along with Matt, Alli and some of the production team. At the village hall there was an unveiling ceremony and when Chris and Gaynor pulled the cord, the red velvet curtains opened and there was not one but two plaques on the wall! The upper one was a beautiful oval shaped tribute to the fan club's 25 years, together with a larger glass framed plaque to be presented to Jenny, who it has to be said was overwhelmed with emotion. It was such a wonderfully proud moment for her and she deserved all of the accolades she received that day. A lovely speech and tribute was paid to Jenny and the club from John Whiston, ITV's Managing Director of Continuing Drama. Afterwards everyone adjourned to the Weetwood Hotel for a special lunch. An absolutely wonderful occasion and a proud day indeed for Jenny and everyone involved with the fan club. Jenny was also presented with a beautiful bouquet of flowers, courtesy of Bryn Dennis Wilson in the hotel restaurant.

Due to filming and hotel commitments, it was decided to celebrate the 25th anniversary club weekend in March 2016. Once again, Matt and his team made it a weekend to remember and the Hollywood theme made it all the more exciting, with the stunning decorations provided by ITV.

Jenny and anniversary plaques at the Village Hall

Jenny was even presented with an 'Oscar' in tribute to her 25 years of dedication to the fan club. A highlight of Jenny's speech was when cast member Michelle Hardwick (Vanessa) took the microphone to proudly tell the assembled crowd that she had applied to join the fan club in her younger years and she went on to tell us how proud she was of the club's achievements and now as an actress in the show, she was delighted to support the fan club whenever she could. Vanessa's heartfelt words brought a great round of applause and Jenny was delighted.

Naomi Rettig was delighted to attend the celebrations and shared these special memories: "My third time at the fan club weekend and the experience just gets better and better. None of my family here at home like Emmerdale (I know, horrific and unbelievable and they're lucky to still be on my Christmas card list) so it's great to get together with fellow cool people who love Emmerdale as much as me. I refer to fellow fan club members as my Emmerdale family and I love the fact that after every visit my family grows as I meet new people, as to me fellow fans make the weekends more enjoyable each time.

Naomi with John Bowe

This weekend was undoubtedly special as it was celebrating the 25th anniversary of the fan club. What an achievement. There's even a plaque now on the village hall to commemorate this, how fabulous is that! The weekend was started with Matt Cleary and Alli Piggott presenting our guru/leader/shining star Jenny Godfrey with a framed award for 25 years of the fan club.

Friday's meet and greet with cast members was extended this year to give us more time to meet everyone. In previous years it had been a bit manic trying to get around to seeing everyone; think speed dating or supermarket sweep. Cast members had come straight from filming to meet us, it was so good of them to give up their time. They were: Bhasker Patel (Rishi), Mark Charnock (Marlon), Zoe Henry (Rhona), Laura Norton (Kerry), Isabel Hodgkins (Victoria), Jeff Hordley (Cain), John Bowe (Lawrence), Ryan Hawley (Robert), Danny Miller (Aaron), Mike Parr (Ross) and Kelvin Fletcher (Andy). It seems everyone loves a bad boy as the queues to see 'Ross', 'Cain' and 'Robert' were the longest! After a delicious meal there was a pub quiz to round the night off, 'The Five Misfits' won (their choice of name not me being rude!) beating 'The Finns' by just one point. Ouch.

Saturday began with a tour of the studios. This is always a favourite of mine, seeing what sets have changed, who's had new décor etc. The attention to detail of the set dressers is a credit to them; it really is as shabby on the Dingles' set as you would imagine! The production crew were dotted around each studio ready to answer any questions, I love finding out how they got to work on Emmerdale and what they all do. This year was special as 4 volunteers were needed from each mini group (we were split into 5 groups) to act out a scene and have it filmed by the crew. I volunteered and played Moira in my group. It was such a fun experience and I really enjoyed it. When we all came back together as one group at the end we got to watch all 5 scenes, everyone was a great sport and we had many laughs, although I think the Butler's Farm door will need to be reinforced after having 5 enthusiastic Ross Barton's bursting through it! While at the studios we had an interesting and informative talk by two ladies from the costume department and we also took a tour of the Props department, where we saw where each characters' items are kept when not on set.

After lunch at the studios we headed back to the hotel where we could buy some merchandise – I was very excited to buy a hessian shopping bag from David's shop, before relaxing and getting ready for the gala dinner and dance. There was a lovely surprise meeting with Dominic Brunt (Paddy) who couldn't make either evening but had turned up off the cuff at the hotel to meet any fans that were milling about. Again, how good of him to give up his time for us fans.

The theme for this year's evening was 'Hollywood glamour' and everyone had made such an effort to look glitzy, we could all have graced the 'Oscars' red carpet with ease. We had the chance to meet and greet cast members throughout the evening. Attending were: Bhasker Patel (Rishi), Elizabeth Estensen (Diane), Chris Chittell (Eric), Gillian Kearney (Emma), Liam Fox (Dan), Steve Halliwell (Zak), Michelle Hardwick (Vanessa), Natalie J

Robb (Moira), Gaynor Faye (Megan), and John Middleton (Ashley). After a scrumptious meal, charity auction and raffle there was an Elvis tribute artist to kick start the dancing off and a disco in between his sets. In the Hollywood theme there were masks of actors on the tables and being the excitable child I am I had to run around the tables having photos of myself being the stars, good fun and I think I made a very good Jim Carey. Everyone had a fun time dancing the night away until well past midnight with Gaynor, Michelle and Liam being the hard core dancers of the cast.

Sunday was the trip to the village outdoor set. My mum asks me if I get bored of seeing the village as it doesn't change. Of course I don't! Who could get bored in the village, it's such a beautiful place to be, and I want to buy one of the new Mill apartments so I could stay forever! And even though the buildings don't change other things do. David's shop front has had its make-over with his new van outside, the door to the vets was open for us to peek in (that's one of the sets actually filmed in the village rather than in the studio), the Dingle's van was parked up for us to have photos with and there were the new graves to look at in the graveyard! And of course there was the fan club plaque on the village hall to see. Oh, and a new tractor in the playground which brought out my inner five-year-old (and the others I saw sitting on it!)

After a splendid carvery back at the hotel it was time to say goodbye – the worst part of the weekend, leaving the Emmerdale bubble. But I left with more friends to add to my Emmerdale family, I learnt a little Swedish, and I feel like one of the luckiest people ever. Thank you to everyone who made the weekend wonderful; Jenny, Matt, Alli, the cast, the crew, and fellow fan club members. And housekeeping at the hotel who removed two spindly spiders for me".

Brendan and Kathy Wright were on their first ever club weekend for the Hollywood style celebrations: "We have watched Emmerdale since it first started and always wondered how we would get to see the current village setting (after visiting Arncliffe and Esholt many years ago). We thoroughly enjoyed the weekend and it certainly exceeded all of our expectations. As first time 'weekenders', having only joined the fan club a few months before the event, we were over the moon to get an allocation for the weekend in March 2016. We both thought the entire event was a fantastic experience and very well organized.

We were amazed at the number of Emmerdale cast members that we came into contact with on both the Friday and Saturday evenings. We loved everything including the hotel, the food, the room, the staff, the visit to the studios, the village and the gala dinner, where everyone including Chris Chittell added that special touch. Brilliant!"

Kathy and Brendan ready to party!

Paul Dacombe joined the fan club in 2015 and attended the 25th anniversary weekend. Paul is a keen photographer and artist and said: "I've watched Emmerdale on and off for longer than I can remember but became an avid viewer when my favourite actor, Danny Miller returned to the show in 2014.

I only became a fan club member in 2015 and attended my first club weekend in 2016. It was an absolutely amazing experience, particularly as I hadn't expected to meet so many of the cast including some of the legends, Steve Halliwell (Zak), Chris Chittell (Eric) and Elizabeth Estensen (Diane) and some newer favourites, Ryan Hawley

Paul with Danny Miller

(Robert) and of course Danny Miller (Aaron). It was fascinating visiting the studios, and in the village I was able to indulge my passion for photography, taking photos of the iconic buildings and scenery. I met some lovely fans too and I helped Angie with some photos she wanted for the book so it was a brilliant weekend in many different ways.

As a fan of Danny Miller, last year I became aware of the charity that Danny had co-founded called 'Once Upon A Smile' in memory of the late Gavin Blythe, and I became a supporter of the charity (mainly attending charity football matches). At the events I had the pleasure of meeting Danny and others from Emmerdale who took part including Joe Gill (Finn), Anthony Quinlan (Pete), Kelvin Fletcher (Andy) and Mike Parr (Ross).

Jenny, Bryn and lovely bouquet

I have always loved drawing and so far have managed to draw some of the actors including Danny and I was delighted when Jenny included the drawing in a recent newsletter. I sent the original to Danny at the studios. I have also provided Angie with a drawing of Shirley Stelfox (Edna) who sadly passed away earlier this year. Shirley was a mainstay of the show for many years and I wanted to pay tribute to her and felt a drawing would be the best way for me to do so.

Thanks to Jenny and all the cast and crew who work so hard to give the fans a special weekend they will never forget. Thank you everyone and long live the fan club!"

The final encore has to be from **Jenny**, who made the fan club dream a reality: "I would like to thank Angie for publishing this book. It is a lovely tribute to the club and its members. It also shows how much Emmerdale acknowledge and appreciate their fans.

Over the years we have been disappointed that the show has not received the credit it deserves in the TV Soap Awards, so we are delighted that after 18 years, Emmerdale was the winner of 'Best Soap' in 2016.

Hollywood Glitz!

The help I have had from Matt and the crew at Emmerdale has been totally invaluable and the fan club would simply not have been the force it is without the co-operation of the ITV staff. At this point I would like to extend special thanks to Alli Piggott who has done everything anyone could possibly do to make our weekends so memorable, and been there for me whenever I have needed help with whatever was needed for the fan club.

I am very proud of our club and the fan club family that has been created from our love of Emmerdale. To all the members around the world, thank you for sharing this wonderful journey spanning 25 years and more. I hope to see many of you again very soon to enjoy even more fan club events".

Drawing of Danny Miller by Paul Dacombe

Acknowledgements

Writing this book has been an absolute joy, not least because of the love and generosity of spirit shown to me whilst gathering the information I needed to produce this special tribute.

To Matt Cleary, Alli Piggott and the cast and crew at ITV studios in Leeds who have given their time, enthusiasm and love to support this project – thank you all, it would not have been possible without you. Special thanks also to Chris Chittell and Gaynor Faye for agreeing to feature on the front cover – a lovely show of support.

To Jenny, our fan club founder, this book is dedicated to you and the wonderful fan club you have created for all of us. For 25 years you have made dreams come true for the members, enriching our lives with the special camaraderie of 'The Emmerdale Club'.

To the fan club members who have shown just how much they love the show with their wonderful and heartfelt accounts of the friendships they have made with fellow fans over the last 25 years. Thanks to all of you.

Finally, a special thank you to club member Paul Dacombe who weaved his photographic magic with photographs and drawings for the book – often at very short notice!

Thanks to each and every one of you – 'The Emmerdale family'.

Fan Club Membership

If you would like to join the 'The Emmerdale Club',
you can download an application form on the ITV website at
www.itv.com/emmerdale/about/fan-club or write to:

The Emmerdale Club
P O Box 330
St Albans
Hertfordshire
AL4 0LF

GALLERY OF FANS